THE
NEW YORK
SUBWAY
SYSTEM

BUILDING
HISTORY
SERIES

THE
NEW YORK
SUBWAY
SYSTEM

by Tim McNeese

Lucent Books, Inc., San Diego, California

TITLES IN THE BUILDING HISTORY SERIES INCLUDE:

The Great Wall of China
The New York Subway System
The Panama Canal
The Pyramids of Giza

Library of Congress Cataloging-in-Publication Data

McNeese, Tim.
    The New York subway system / by Tim McNeese.
        p.   cm. — (Building history series)
    Includes bibliographical references and index.
    Summary: Discusses the history of the New York City subway
system.
    ISBN 1-56006-427-7 (alk. paper)
    1. Subways—New York (State)—New York—Juvenile
literature. [1. Subways—New York (State)—New York.] I. Title.
II. Series.
  TF847.N5M38   1997
  388.4'28'097471—dc21   96-48700
                                                                                                    CIP
                                                                                                    AC

Copyright 1997 by Lucent Books, Inc.
P.O. Box 289011, San Diego, California 92198-9011

Printed in the U.S.A.

CONTENTS

FOREWORD   6

IMPORTANT DATES IN THE BUILDING OF THE
    NEW YORK SUBWAY SYSTEM   8

INTRODUCTION   10

CHAPTER ONE
    Beyond the Sidewalks: New York's
    Early Mass Transit   14

CHAPTER TWO
    To Harlem in Fifteen Minutes: Building
    New York's First Subway, 1900–1904   30

CHAPTER THREE
    Underground Partnership: The IRT
    and BRT Expand the Line   50

CHAPTER FOUR
    The IND: New York's Last Great Line   67

CHAPTER FIVE
    New Yorkers and Their Subway   77

    For Further Reading   87
    Works Consulted   89
    Index   91
    Picture Credits   95
    About the Author   96

FOREWORD

Throughout history, as civilizations have evolved and prospered, each has produced unique buildings and architectural styles. Combining the need for both utility and artistic expression, a society's buildings, particularly its large-scale public structures, often reflect the individual character traits that distinguish it from other societies. In a very real sense, then, buildings express a society's values and unique characteristics in tangible form. As scholar Anita Abromovitz comments in her book *People and Spaces*, "Our ways of living and thinking—our habits, needs, fear of enemies, aspirations, materialistic concerns, and religious beliefs—have influenced the kinds of spaces that we build and that later surround and include us."

That specific types and styles of structures constitute an outward expression of the spirit of an individual people or era can be seen in the diverse ways that various societies have built palaces, fortresses, tombs, churches, government buildings, sports arenas, public works, and other such monuments. The ancient Greeks, for instance, were a supremely rational people who originated Western philosophy and science, including the atomic theory and the realization that the earth is a sphere. Their public buildings, epitomized by Athens's magnificent Parthenon temple, were equally rational, emphasizing order, harmony, reason, and above all, restraint.

By contrast, the Romans, who conquered and absorbed the Greek lands, were a highly practical people preoccupied with acquiring and wielding power over others. The Romans greatly admired and readily copied elements of Greek architecture, but modified and adapted them to their own needs. "Roman genius was called into action by the enormous practical needs of a world empire," wrote historian Edith Hamilton. "Rome met them magnificently. Buildings tremendous, indomitable, amphitheaters where eighty thousand could watch a spectacle, baths where three thousand could bathe at the same time."

In medieval Europe, God heavily influenced and motivated the people, and religion permeated all aspects of society, molding people's worldviews and guiding their everyday actions. That spiritual mindset is reflected in the most important medieval structure—the Gothic cathedral—which, in a sense, was a model of heavenly cities. As scholar Anne Fremantle so elegantly phrases it, the cathedrals were "harmonious elevations of stone and glass reaching up to heaven to seek and receive the light [of God]."

Our more secular modern age, in contrast, is driven by the realities of a global economy, advanced technology, and mass communications. Responding to the needs of international trade and the growth of cities housing millions of people, today's builders construct engineering marvels, among them towering skyscrapers of steel and glass, mammoth marine canals, and huge and elaborate rapid transit systems, all of which would have left their ancestors, even the Romans, awestruck.

In examining some of humanity's greatest edifices, Lucent Books' Building History Series recognizes this close relationship between a society's historical character and its buildings. Each volume in the series begins with a historical sketch of the people who erected the edifice, exploring their major achievements as well as the beliefs, customs, and societal needs that dictated the variety, functions, and styles of their buildings. A detailed explanation of how the selected structure was conceived, designed, and built, to the extent that this information is known, makes up the majority of the volume.

Each volume in the Lucent Building History Series also includes several special features that are useful tools for additional research. A chronology of important dates gives students an overview, at a glance, of the evolution and use of the structure described. Sidebars create a broader context by adding further details on some of the architects, engineers, and construction tools, materials, and methods that made each structure a reality, as well as the social, political, and/or religious leaders and movements that inspired its creation. Useful maps help the reader locate the nations, cities, streets, and individual structures mentioned in the text; and numerous diagrams and pictures illustrate tools and devices that bring to life various stages of construction. Finally, each volume contains two bibliographies, one for student research, the other listing works the author consulted in compiling the book.

Taken as a whole, these volumes, covering diverse ancient and modern structures, constitute not only a valuable research tool, but also a tribute to the human spirit, a fascinating exploration of the dreams, skills, ingenuity, and dogged determination of the great peoples who shaped history.

IMPORTANT DATES IN THE BUILDING OF THE NEW YORK SUBWAY SYSTEM

1900

February 21—Financier August Belmont signs contract with city of New York to build the Interborough Rapid Transit Company's first subway.

March 24—Grand celebration marks the beginning of construction of the IRT's first subway miles.

1899

Board of Rapid Transit Railroad Commissioners (RTC) takes bids for construction of New York's first official subway system.

1904

October 27, official opening and dedication of the first nine miles of IRT-constructed subway.

| 1895 | 1900 | 1905 | 1910 | 1915 | 1920 |

1902

January 27 dynamite accident caused by careless subway worker destroys several city blocks, killing 7 people and injuring over 180.

1913

New York's Public Service Commission issues the Dual Contracts, signed by the IRT and the BRT, on March 19.

Interior of the City Hall Station, 1904.

1905

Daily ridership on the New York subway tops 600,000.

1922
New York mayor
John F. Hylan an-
nounces his plan
for a city-owned
and city-operated
subway system
(the IND).

Subway riders, 1950.

1947
Annual ridership
on the New York
City subway sys-
tem reaches the
2 billion mark.

1932
September 10, official opening and dedication of the IND
subway line.

1925	1930	1935	1940	1945	1950

1925
March 14, groundbreaking for
the first construction of the IND
subway line.

1946
All-time record for
number of passengers
in a single twenty-
four-hour period set
December 23:
8,872,244.

1940
June 1—The Brooklyn-Manhattan
Transit Corporation (BMT) be-
comes the property of the city of
New York.

June 12—The Interborough Rapid
Transit Company (IRT) becomes
the property of the city of New
York.

INTRODUCTION

Beneath the busy commercial and residential streets of the most populous urban center in America, New York City, lies the most extensive mass transit system in the world. The New York City subway system is the longest underground transportation system of them all, its tunnels extending throughout all five boroughs, or urban districts—Manhattan, Brooklyn, Bronx, Queens, and Staten Island—for a combined length of 722 miles of busy track. The system moves the lifeblood of the city, taking people to and from their jobs, their homes, their businesses. Author-historian Brian Cudahy, writing in *Under the Sidewalks of New York*, explains how elaborate the New York subway system is:

> How can one begin to speak about the New York subway, an urban railway network of almost unfathomable dimensions? . . . If the subway tokens [passengers] drop in the turnstiles in one day were stacked one on top of

THE FIVE BOROUGHS OF NEW YORK CITY

Long Island Sound

BRONX

Hudson River

East River

MANHATTAN

QUEENS

Upper New York Bay

BROOKLYN

Jamaica Bay

STATEN ISLAND

Lower New York Bay

Rockaway Inlet

North Atlantic Ocean

The streets of New York City are crowded with horse-drawn wagons in this 1886 lithograph. The population explosion of the nineteenth century created extreme congestion and the need for new mass transit systems.

another, they would tower 21,000 feet into the air—a genuine menace for aerial navigation. Placed edge-to-edge along the ground, they would extend from Times Square to Bridgeport, Connecticut. The system provides work for over 20,000 employees, requires a fleet of 6,500 subway cars to meet daily schedules, and spends about 100 million dollars each year just for electricity!

While New York's subway is not the oldest (London's Underground was built forty years earlier), it is one of the busiest. Clifton Hood, author of *722 Miles: The Building of the Subways and How They Transformed New York*, notes the system's importance:

On average, more than 2.7 million New Yorkers ride the underground railway every day. The subway figures so prominently in New York City's daily life that it has been represented in movies, paintings, plays, songs, dances, and other forms of popular culture ever since the first line opened in 1904. . . . New York City's subway is the longest rapid transit system in the world, larger than the London underground, the Paris metro, the Tokyo subway, and the Seoul subway. If its tracks were laid end to end, the subway would stretch from Manhattan to Chicago. . . . It is so immense that it has a 4,250-person police force . . . which is larger than the entire police departments of such American cities as Boston, Atlanta, St. Louis, Dallas, Denver, and San Francisco.

The subway system was spawned by the tremendous growth that took place in New York City during the nineteenth century. New York opened the century with a population hovering around sixty thousand, and most of its citizens lived on the southern tip of Manhattan Island. By the end of the nineteenth century the city's population had grown to nearly 3.5 million.

Subway riders at the Lexington Avenue and 42nd Street station unload from trains while others anxiously crowd aboard. During the 1940s, an estimated 2.3 billion passengers used the New York City Transit System every year.

Building the giant subway system took several decades, but most construction spanned the years between 1900 and 1940. The city of New York provided most of the money for the subway construction, expending hundreds of millions of dollars. Designed originally to alleviate overcrowding on New York's existing mass transit carriers—such as streetcars and horse carts—the subway soon became the most popular and inexpensive means of travel.

By 1940, ridership on the New York City Transit System was 2.3 *billion* passengers annually. Throughout nearly a century of service, the New York City subway has provided a vital service to its citizens and to the city's visitors by providing hundreds of miles of subway lines throughout the five boroughs. And through the years, the purpose of the subway has remained elemental: to get people where they need to go.

BEYOND THE SIDEWALKS: NEW YORK'S EARLY MASS TRANSIT

During the first half of the nineteenth century, New York City boomed. Between 1840 and 1860, New York's population increased from 300,000 to over 800,000, a 167 percent increase in just twenty years. The primary cause of this great population growth was immigration. Hundreds of thousands of Europeans streamed into the United States from the 1820s through the 1850s, dramatically swelling urban centers such as Boston, Philadelphia, and especially New York. On the city's streets, stagecoaches called omnibuses and small horse-drawn wagons provided the only mass transit of the day. The state of public transportation at midcentury was woefully inadequate, even dangerous. Historian-writer Robert Daley describes an all-too-common scene on New York's streets:

> No tracks hampered the operations of the stages, whose drivers ran over men, women and children in their haste to beat competitors to waiting passengers. Burly conductors shanghaied people into coaches and forced them to pay, so that heavy profits could be shown. Drivers were picked for heft not courtesy. Most swore at the passengers, and swindled them on tickets and on change. Axles broke, horses shied and policemen on boxes at intersections spent more time separating slugging rival drivers than directing snarled traffic.

Clearly, something had to be done to help relieve the traffic congestion. Rail service was introduced to Manhattan Island by the 1860s, but it provided only temporary relief. Then in 1864, Hugh B. Willson, a railroad entrepreneur from Michigan, presented as a solution the construction of a subway line beneath the streets of Manhattan.

Willson soon began financing his own company, the Metropolitan Railway Company, taking on a construction engineer, A. P. Robinson, as his partner. Robinson proposed the construction of tunnels close to the surface of the streets to save money. Robinson's plan was to build the tunnels using the straightforward "cut-and-cover" method, which would require tearing up the streets, excavating long troughs below street level, and resurfacing the streets to cover the tunnel. He touted the effectiveness and efficiency of his proposed system:

> There would be no dust, there would be no mud. Passengers . . . have simply to enter a station from the sidewalk and pass down a spacious and well-lighted staircase to a dry and roomy platform. The temperature would be cool in summer and warm in winter. There would be no delays from snow or ice. The cars would not be obliged to wait for a lazy or obstinate truckman.

Coaches line the streets of New York City's Madison Square while cab drivers wait for passengers. Intense competition existed among the drivers; in addition to frequent brawls with rival cabbies, drivers would also abduct passengers and then force them to pay for the ride.

The passenger would be sure of a luxurious seat in a well-lighted car, and would be carried to his destination in one-third the time he could be carried by any other conveyance. These would be the advantages to those who ride.

However, despite the benefits such a subway system might have offered the city, Willson and Robinson faced immediate opposition. There was widespread doubt of the safety of such an underground rail system. But the greatest obstacle Willson and his partner faced came from one man: William Marcy Tweed, popularly known to the citizens of New York as "Boss" Tweed.

Boss Tweed dominated New York City politics. Through his political cronies and backroom connections, Tweed controlled many of the political decisions affecting New York's present and future operations. As the city's commissioner of public works, he collected fees from omnibus and horse cart operators for licensing their vehicles. Thus, Tweed saw a subway as direct competition to his street vehicles.

William "Boss" Tweed

In March 1864, a bill to allow construction of a New York City subway was introduced in the New York State legislature on Willson's behalf. In the spring of 1865, however, Governor Ruben E. Fenton, a friend of Tweed's, vetoed the bill. The following year, Willson made a second failed attempt at chartering a subway line for New York City.

CHARLES HARVEY AND THE EL

While Willson and Robinson fought for their dream of New York's first underground railroad, another entrepreneur was working on a completely different solution to the transportation crisis. An inventor named Charles T. Harvey began designing a railway line that would relieve street traffic by literally rising above it. Harvey's idea was for the building of an elevated rail line that ran along wrought iron supports. The line was to be

Inventor Charles T. Harvey drives a small railway car atop the new West Side and Yonkers Patent Railway in this 1867 photograph.

an elevated cable car railroad. Had Tweed opposed it, it too probably would have died. But Tweed saw no chance for success for the elevated line and so did not oppose it. Harvey received approval from the New York State legislature in 1867. Construction began on July 1, 1867, on his West Side and Yonkers Patent Railway.

Within six months, the first quarter mile of the elevated line was open for business. By the following July, another quarter mile had been completed. The future for Harvey's elevated line looked promising. However, on September 26, 1869, a banking crisis signaled the beginning of a nationwide depression that crippled the banking industry and lost Harvey his financial backing. He finally found support from a group of Wall Street investors who agreed to finance him in exchange for control of his railroad, but the partnership did not last long. Harvey was

Elevated railways were built throughout New York City during the late 1800s. Although the els relieved some of the street traffic, they failed to solve New York's transit dilemma.

soon voted off the board of directors. Reorganized, the line re-opened in 1871 as the New York Elevated Railway, soon nick-named "the el."

Construction proceeded and within four years the line had been extended to Central Park. During the summer of 1875 more than 170,000 New Yorkers were passengers. By 1876, the el was carrying twice that number, and other entrepreneurs were building interconnected els above the cityscape of New York.

In 1883, an additional rapid transit line linking Manhattan and Brooklyn began operation with the opening of the new Brooklyn Bridge. Stretching across the length of the bridge was a cable-operated train, which proved to be highly popular. A year after it was put into service, the cable train carried over 9 million passengers back and forth from Manhattan to Brooklyn. Over the next five years, three additional els stretched up and down the main boulevards of Brooklyn. However, despite the proliferation of elevated train lines from Manhattan to Brooklyn in the latter decades of the nineteenth century, the el failed to solve the city's mass transit problems. The streets had become crowded with elevated tracks, builders were running out of space, and the population of New York (and therefore its mass transit ridership) was still growing fast. Clearly, something had to be done. In 1888, the mayor of New York City, Abram S. Hewitt, went before the city's board of aldermen and made a proposal designed to solve New York's mass transit problem: Build a subway.

THE DREAM TAKES SHAPE

The speech Abram Hewitt delivered on January 31, 1888, to the city aldermen had one clear message: Despite the success and popularity of the mass transit systems in place in New York by that year, the entire system of horse cars, omnibuses, and elevated rail lines was woefully inadequate. The city needed, in Hewitt's estimation, an advanced mass transit system, and soon. Hewitt's plan for a new rapid transit system was a simple one. Often referred to as the "Hewitt formula," the plan called for the city of New York to arrange the financing for the new subway system and retain ownership of it.

In 1883, a cable-operated train was built across the new Brooklyn Bridge. Over 9 million passengers used the popular railway during its first year in operation.

BEACH'S SECRET SUBWAY

Despite his best efforts, Boss Tweed was unable to block the building of at least one underground line in New York City during his reign as political controller in the 1860s and 1870s. In fact, this subway system was constructed without Tweed's even being aware of its existence. The man responsible was Alfred Ely Beach, an inventor, engineer, newspaper publisher, and creative genius.

From the beginning, Beach's plan called for the construction of a pneumatic tube, through which a subway car could be pushed by a powerful blast of forced air generated by an enormous fan system. As Beach worked on his subway designs, he imagined a rounded tube and a subway car that would fit snugly into the tube.

Beach then began considering just how such a tunnel could be dug under the streets of New York. Ever the inventor, Beach emerged from his tinkering having invented a great hydraulic shield, a drill that bored seventeen inches into the earth with each forward surge, all the while protecting the diggers who worked from within the shield itself. Others could follow behind the device, building the brick walls for the pneumatic subway tube.

But Beach realized that before he could begin construction, he would have to pay off Tweed with large sums of money. Beach could not bring himself to pay the bribes, telling his brother: "I won't pay political blackmail. I say, let's build the subway furtively." Thus began one of the most fascinating building schemes in the history of New York.

In 1869, he rented the cellar of Devlin's Clothing Store on the corner of Murray Street and Broadway. From inside the basement wall, Beach ordered his men, including his twenty-year-old son, Fred, to begin digging. Historian Stan Fischler describes the work:

> Claustrophobia was a persistent problem. Fear that the horses galloping overhead, whose hoofbeats were acutely audible in the tunnel, would crash through and expose the project constantly weighed on the workers. Many quit and never returned. Others worked apprehensively in the close [dank and humid] tunnel air, guided by lantern light, pecking away at the dirt and sand.

Beach's subway, measuring 312 feet in length, was finally introduced to the public on February 26, 1870. His subway was an amazingly ornate project. He spent $350,000 constructing the line and furnishing the two subterranean stations at both ends. In one station he installed a grand piano, lavish decorations, an aquarium, and a bubbling fountain, the entire works illuminated by the light of zircon lamps. To push his single subway car through the tunnel, Beach installed an immense fan system called the Roots Patent Force Blast Blower, a contraption capable of sending the car through the tube at a top speed of ten miles an hour. Invited city officials and reporters were stunned by the scene they found beneath the streets of Boss Tweed's New York. Each took a ride in the twenty-two-passenger car, marveling at its roominess, cleanliness, and lavishness.

Beach intended to build more tunnels to a total length of five miles running up and down the length of Manhattan Island. He approached the state legislature for a subway charter. However, since New York's governor, John T. Hoffman, was pro-Tweed, he squelched Beach's plan in support of his political crony.

In 1872, Beach resubmitted his proposal. Public doubt about wind power's ability to push a subway train for several miles led Beach to replace his pneumatic tube technology with steam power. In 1873 the Beach Transit bill won approval of the legislature and the new state governor. However, financial backers never materialized. The great subway envisioned by Beach for so many years would never be built. In time, he closed his short subway line and soon the public forgot about it.

Forty years later, however, a crew of subway construction workers digging a new Broadway line accidentally broke into Beach's old, abandoned line. Astonished, they examined the mysterious brick-lined tunnel and its magnificent stations. Beach had left nearly everything intact when he closed the system decades earlier, including his single subway car, which still sat on its tracks as if ready to deliver its next group of passengers down the long-abandoned and darkened tunnel.

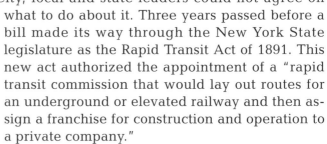

Despite the rapid proliferation of elevated railways, New York's mass transit systems could not accommodate the growing population. Many people believed an underground railway, or subway, would solve the city's transportation problems.

Once a company was selected to construct the system, that company would manage the line for profit in a lease arrangement with the city.

Despite the obvious need for a new subway system in New York City, local and state leaders could not agree on what to do about it. Three years passed before a bill made its way through the New York State legislature as the Rapid Transit Act of 1891. This new act authorized the appointment of a "rapid transit commission that would lay out routes for an underground or elevated railway and then assign a franchise for construction and operation to a private company."

By October 1892, the commission had formulated limited early plans providing for a few miles of subway lines running north and south on Manhattan Island. But in late 1892, when the commission opened the building contract up for bids,

Abram S. Hewitt

there were no takers. The nation was slipping into an economic depression and no investor could afford to undertake the costs of a major building project.

ENTER THE RAPID TRANSIT COMMISSION

Stalled by the so-called Panic of 1893, the subway commission dissolved. By 1894, a new subway commission called the Board of Rapid Transit Railroad Commissioners (known as the RTC) was formed. Spearheading the commission was one of the best-known and most talented design engineers of his day, William Barclay Parsons. He would prove to be invaluable to the design and construction of the city's new subway. After much delay concerning route changes and financing issues, by November 1899 the RTC was ready to take bids on construction of a Manhattan Island subway.

The commission received only two bids. John B. McDonald, a fifty-five-year-old Irish immigrant from New York, won the contract with a bid of $35 million. McDonald had more than thirty years of construction experience, including work on the Croton Dam, a project that helped provide the water supply for the city of New York. He had also built railroads, including a portion of the New York Central, which featured a four-track system of tunnels. Since all subways of the day were basically railroads built underground, such experience was deemed essential to this mass transit project.

McDonald's many years of engineering experience paid off during the building of the New York subway. He proved himself capable as well of organizing men and winning their loyalty, moving work along, and keeping the job under budget and on schedule. In addition, he had connections with Tammany Hall, the political headquarters of the city. His fellow Irishmen who ran the great, yet corrupt, system of New York politics proved to be valuable allies for McDonald, who

New York Transit Museum Archives, Brooklyn

City officials contracted with engineer John B. McDonald for the building of the Manhattan Island subway.

occasionally needed to cut hurriedly through legal red tape. In exchange, McDonald provided certain building jobs to favored Tammany Hall supporters.

One qualification McDonald was not able to meet alone was ready funds. Before he could begin building, he had to pay nearly $7 million to the city to clear the way for construction rights. Unable to raise the money, he was forced to surrender his contract to a wealthy banker named August Belmont. Backed by his vast financial resources, Belmont soon signed a new contract with the city of New York, retaining McDonald as his chief building contractor.

The contract, signed on February 21, 1900, required Belmont to "build, equip, and operate the railway for a period of fifty years." In exchange, the city of New York agreed to provide Belmont with $36.5 million for construction costs, including

On February 21, 1900, wealthy banker August Belmont (pictured) became the new subway financier.

A CELEBRATION TO BEGIN THE DIGGING

Thundering cannon boomed their salutes as church bells chimed and Japanese fireworks burst in the skies above New York City. Such was the celebration during the groundbreaking ceremonies held on March 24, 1900, to mark the beginning of construction on the long-awaited New York City subway.

Twenty-five thousand people gathered in a small park across the street from city hall to mark the occasion. The famous bandleader and march composer John Philip Sousa was on hand, conducting his band through a variety of stirring selections. Overseeing the proceedings, which took place on a clear spring day, was the city's mayor, Robert A. Van Wyck, who wielded a wood and silver spade made by Tiffany and Company silversmiths to be used to scoop out the symbolic first shovel of New York earth.

Once Van Wyck had performed his duty, a great tumult of noise and flash hit the skies above New York City. The Pain Fireworks Company of New Jersey launched fireworks with an explosive power

Flags and streamers decorate the city hall building for the subway's groundbreaking ceremony on March 24, 1900.

equal to fifty tons of dynamite. Twenty-one cannon fired a noisy national salute. Pyrotechnicians detonated daylight fireworks that zipped and blasted above the streets, releasing twenty huge "flag bombs" above the crowd, each bomb containing 144 small silk American flags. Thousands of flags filled the sky in this extravagant display.

Mayor Van Wyck capped the event with a speech in which he declared the subway to be one of the greatest construction projects in the history of New York State, second only to the building of the Erie Canal earlier in the nineteenth century. "No Roman citizen," the mayor claimed, "ever entertained a keener pride in the glory of that imperial city than does the New Yorker in the fame of New York." After thirty years of discussion, speculation, and promise, New Yorkers were at last going to see the building of their first underground rapid transit system.

$1.5 million to purchase land for subway stations. When the subway line was completed, Belmont would operate the subway, collecting passenger fees and making lease payments to the city to recoup building costs.

Once Belmont had signed the contract, he formed two companies: the Rapid Transit Subway Construction Company, which would see to the construction of the subway lines, and the Interborough Rapid Transit Company, known as the IRT, which would operate the system once it was built.

THE WORK OF WILLIAM BARCLAY PARSONS

Construction of the subway system came to rely on the efforts of three very different men. Belmont was the financier and figurehead. John McDonald would see to the day-to-day construction of the line. And William Barclay Parsons, the chief engineer for the RTC, experienced in designing rail systems and water supply delivery systems, was soon in charge of designing the new subway system. Writer Clifton Hood describes this great designer of New York's first subway:

> Tall and rangy, with a prominent jaw and piercing eyes that made him appear good-looking in a rough sort of way, Parsons radiated strength and dignity. He stayed calm under pressure and was known for his rigid self-control. Parsons was hardly an amiable or engaging man, and he had little personal warmth. But this stern, demanding patrician nonetheless drew first-rate engineers to his side, inspired their best work, and earned their lifelong loyalty.

The first part of the subway system, completed in 1904, owed much to the design skill, creativity, tenacity, and judgment of William Barclay Parsons.

ELECTRICITY POWERS THE SUBWAY

Among Parsons's important decisions regarding the nature of the new subway system was the choice of the system's power source. Most elevated trains to that date were powered by steam locomotives. Parsons, however, selected electricity to propel the underground system, thus eliminating the smoke, dust, and smell of running steam locomotives underground. In 1887, an inventor and Annapolis graduate named Frank Sprague had

William Barclay Parsons, the RTC's chief engineer, designed New York City's subway system.

designed a successful streetcar system powered by electricity. By the mid-1890s, Sprague had developed a system, called multiple-unit control, that allowed a train engineer or motorman standing in the train's lead car to control the motors of all the cars in his train via one lever. Such a system allowed for uniform speed, control, and braking for a subway train.

DESIGNS FOR THE SUBWAY

When mapping the specific route of the system, Parsons and the RTC decided on a line bisecting Manhattan and extending into the Bronx to the north. The Bronx terminus would be a natural point of future growth on the north end of the island. Author Hood describes the accepted route:

> The route finally decided upon began with a loop near City Hall, proceeded with four tracks up to Grand Central Station, then westward to Broadway and along Broadway to 104th Street. From there one double track line continued along Broadway to Kingsbridge, and

another eastward under the Harlem River through the Bronx to the Zoological Gardens. The total length of the system would be about 21 miles, including 5 miles of el.

William Parsons proposed a series of tunnels to be built near the surface of the streets to a depth of between fifteen or twenty feet. Parsons had seen such a subway design during a visit to Budapest, Hungary. Historian Stan Fischler describes the Hungarian system on which the New York subway was modeled:

> [The] Hungarians [had] simply cut a huge trench along the route of their subway, built their railroad at the bottom, roofed it with steel girders, and used a few feet of fill and paving on top of the roof. This "cut-and-cover" method was eventually to be universally employed in subway construction. It was infinitely cheaper, easier, and faster.

Not only did Parsons adopt the cut-and-cover method of subway construction from the Hungarians, he also borrowed the

Elaborate Hungarian-style kiosks were built for the new subway. Although the structures were extremely decorative, they were also practical and kept rain out of the tunnels.

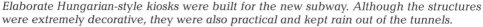

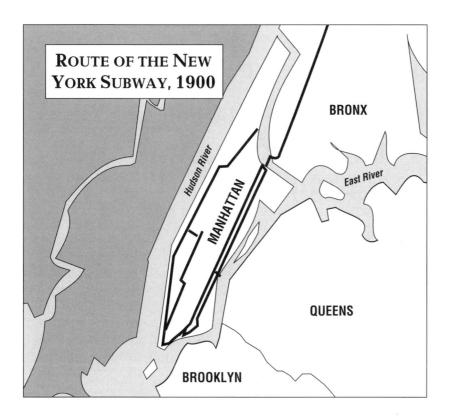

subway station design used in Budapest. Parsons ordered the building of Hungarian kiosks, a design that included a domed roof, which gave the appearance of a Turkish summerhouse of glass and steel. The structures were simultaneously ornamental and functional and were designed to keep rain out of the tunnel below. The Hecla Iron Works manufactured the kiosks, producing 133 of them for the new line.

By the spring of 1900, everything was in place to begin the actual construction of New York City's greatest building project, its subway. The preliminary work of the system's design and route had taken years. Now the contracts had been signed, and the planners of the system were ready to begin the real work. It was the end of a century and the beginning of a new era in the history of New York's mass transit system.

To Harlem in Fifteen Minutes: Building New York's First Subway, 1900–1904

Construction of the first thirteen miles of subterranean tunnels and three miles of elevated track began two days after the groundbreaking ceremony. Although only a few miles in length, this first New York City subway proved to be the beginning of a project that would continue for the next forty years. Little did New Yorkers in 1900 realize that in time their subway system would extend for hundreds of miles beneath the city streets.

The physical demands of the project were extreme. Few large-scale excavating machines were available at the turn of the century. This left the digging to thousands of workers, most of whom were unskilled laborers paid $2 for a ten-hour day; skilled workers received $2.50.

Each mile of tunnel contained the same basic design elements. Typically, a tunnel built by the cut-and-cover method measured approximately fifty-five feet wide. Four tracks were laid side by side to accommodate multiple trains. The tracks themselves resembled aboveground railroad tracks. Hundred-pound rails laid across hard pine cross ties were held in place by steel spikes. Where tunnel and track curved, workers constructed guardrails to help keep subway trains from jumping the track. The wood cross ties were laid on a bed of crushed stone. Beneath it all—rails, cross ties, and stone ballast—was a poured concrete slab floor to give the rail lines greater stability and to minimize seepage and flooding. A cement wall divided the track lines into two sets of two, separating trains running in opposite directions and serving as a "crash wall" in case a train slipped its track.

The cut-and-cover method was the predominant but not sole construction method. Topography and engineering considerations sometimes dictated alternatives. For example, concrete-lined tunnels and cast iron tubes were installed under the East River and Harlem River. About five miles of elevated tracks emerged from tunnels to carry the road on steel viaducts or bridges where the curve and dip of the landscape made tunneling or cut-and-cover either impractical or too expensive.

Most of this mass transit system was to be constructed underground, so lighting the tunnels was an important facet of building the line. Parsons's cut-and-cover tunnels were close enough to the surface of the street that holes could be bored into the tunnel roofs and filled with deadlights—solid glass cylinders that allowed daylight to illuminate the tunnels below. In addition, light-colored ceramic tiles often lined the walls of subway stations, reflecting the filtered street light. In those subway tunnels far below street level, electric lights were strung along the walls of stations, adding illumination by day and providing the only light by night.

A glimpse inside the 15th Street and 4th Avenue tunnel reveals the cut-and-cover construction method.

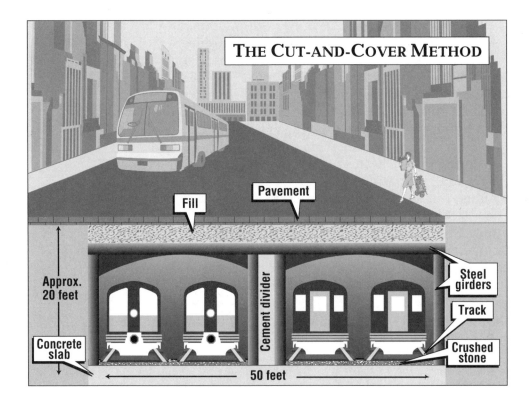

THE CUT-AND-COVER METHOD

Fill

Pavement

Approx. 20 feet

Concrete slab

Cement divider

Steel girders

Track

Crushed stone

50 feet

SUBTERRANEAN BARRIERS

Underground Manhattan provided subway workers with endless challenges. In some places, they encountered great sections of loose, sandy soil or water-soaked loam that practically fell into their hands. Such soil was too unstable for the construction of subway lines, so routes had to be adjusted. At other sites, workers faced hard rock formations that required extensive drilling and dynamiting.

Subway workers often encountered another natural barrier, water. Beneath New York's streets were a variety of water systems, both ancient and modern, many of which could potentially flood subway tunnels. There were underground springs, streams, and even ponds. Some of the water obstacles uncovered by subway workers had once been on the surface of Manhattan Island, long before massive brick and steel buildings drove them underground. Diggers uncovered a sunfish pond at the corner of 32nd Street and Madison Avenue. At Mulberry and Baxter Streets, workers exposed a mineral spring once visited by the sick for its curative properties. Most of these underground aquatic discoveries had long since become polluted.

A tangled maze of man-made obstacles also complicated the work. Workers had to contend with sewer lines and water pipes, as well as gas mains, telephone lines, steam pipes, telegraph wires, electrical conduits, and pneumatic mail tubes. All these systems had to be either bypassed, rerouted, or completely rebuilt to accommodate the construction of the subway lines. Historian Benson Bobrick describes the challenge:

> At Bleecker and Greene the first order of business was to build 900 feet of new 4-foot-diameter brick sewers at a depth of from 1 to 30 feet. Over the years the old pipes and sewers had been laid in a mass without plan, as tangled as fern roots in a wood. Water pipes, thickly encrusted with filth, were discovered running through sewers; great tubes were dug up whose presence was wholly unexplained. In all, 45 miles of conduits would eventually have to be relaid.

Sometimes the men working underground on the subway uncovered other, more exotic objects. They were constantly digging up colonial-era relics, including weapons, tools, household items, and even an occasional chest of coins left behind as buried treasure by some forgotten early citizen of New York. Perhaps the most intriguing find was the remains of a Dutch ship, the *Tiger*, which burned and sank in 1613. Near the Dyckman Street Station, workers unearthed ancient mastodon bones.

ACCIDENTS AND MISHAPS

Since the work of constructing the subway involved digging underground, excavating stone and earth by the ton, and setting explosive charges to cut through hard rock formations, subway workers constantly risked mishaps and accidents. Cave-ins and explosions, though not common, were usually deadly. One cave-in near Park Avenue destroyed enough of the city block between 37th and 38th Streets that August Belmont paid $1 million to purchase the block rather than face a series of lawsuits brought by local New Yorkers seeking damages.

Perhaps the most serious accident took place on January 27, 1902. A powderman named Moses Epps entered a dynamite

Spectators and workmen gather around the site of a cave-in during the building of the 4th Avenue subway. Although cave-ins were rare, their results were often deadly.

storage shed to take his lunch break. To warm his hands in the winter cold, Epps lit a candle in the shed a few feet from more than five hundred pounds of dynamite. Without thinking, Epps left the shed and the candle unattended. In his absence, the candle fell over and caught his lunch wrapper on fire. When he came back to the shed, Epps was horrified to discover spreading flames. After flinging a bucket of water on the fire, Epps ran out of the shed to fetch another pail. Before he could return, the flames were out of control.

Less than a minute later, a huge explosion rocked the work site and the surrounding streets. The blast was so intense that, blocks away, the clocks in the tower of Grand Central Station were blown in. Along 41st Street, debris flew in every direction. Several workers and pedestrians were killed and hundreds were hurt by the blast. The restaurant of the nearby Murray Hill Hotel was crowded for lunch. The explosion rocked the hotel, throwing the diners from their chairs, as deadly shards of window glass flew through the air, cutting down innocent bystanders. A local hospital suffered so much damage that it could not help those injured by the explosion. In all, the blast killed 7 people and injured over 180. As for Epps, he escaped with a few cuts and bruises. After the accident, New York mayor Seth Low ordered the creation of a new city agency, the Municipal Explosives Commission, to regulate the handling of dynamite by subway workers in the future. Blame for the accident fell on Ira A. Shaler, Epps's boss: After investigation of negligence, a grand jury indicted Shaler for manslaughter. Shaler served no jail time, however, and was himself killed in a later cave-in.

Interference with Street Business

As work on the subway advanced, discontent grew among New York City's merchants and businessmen. This type of subway construction required the tearing up of entire blocks of city streets, an annoyance at best and a source of concern and anger when the resulting loss of business on those usually busy blocks harmed merchants and shopkeepers.

Black-and-white photographs of subway work sites reveal the difficulties for merchants, pedestrians, and street-level traffic. Pictured are whole streets, from curb to curb, in total

Workers dig through the rubble of a subway tunnel following a devastating cave-in. The building of the subway required the tearing up of streets from one sidewalk to the other, as this photograph illustrates.

SUBWAY STATIONS

Since their miles of track are buried underground, most portions of most subways are never actually seen by their passengers. Indeed, the only places on the subway passengers view clearly are the stations, where they spend time buying tokens and stand about waiting for the next train. When plans and contracts were drawn up for the New York subway, the appearance of its stations was an important issue. According to one clause of one contract, "All parts of the structure where exposed to public sight shall therefore be designed, constructed, and maintained with a view to the beauty of their appearance, as well as to their efficiency."

At the City Hall Station, a combination of bricks, stained glass, and vaulted ceilings created a unique design.

Forty-eight stations were built on the first New York subway. Of those, thirty-three were constructed underground. Eleven others were included on the el sections of the subway, where the tracks emerged from underground, three were built "partly on the surface and partly underground," and the last was built "partly on the surface and partly on the viaduct."

While the stations had many similarities, they were not exact copies of one another. Often, individual stations were designed around the space available at a given work site. Typically, these stations featured platforms that extended along the subway tracks for 200 to 350 feet. Platforms were typically about 16 feet wide. The station floors were poured concrete, divided into squares, adding to the consistent geometry of the New York subway. Stations featured repeated patterns of parallel lines, including rows of I-beams and ceiling girders, patterned walls of fired ceramic tiles, and the ever-present tracks, with their endless rows of ties and perpendicular iron rails which emerged from the ends of two darkened tunnels.

A few exceptions to this rule did exist. The City Hall Station, for example, featured an elaborate brick-and-stone arched entrance, as well as a vaulted ceiling of brick laid in a zigzag pattern. At the peak of the station's three-domed vault were filigreed circles of stained glass skylights, which

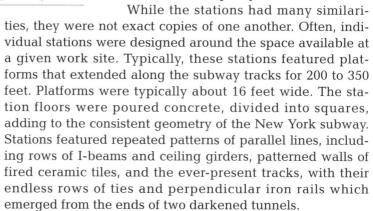

allowed patterned, colored street light to filter in above the oak ticket counter. In this station, the subway rails curved gently, causing a break in the usual pattern of straight lines and uniform repetition of space. The City Hall Station platform curved alongside the tracks. This combination of arches, vaults, and domed ceilings gave this station a look uniquely its own. The station's architects were Heins and La Farge, designers of New York City's arched Cathedral Church of St. John the Divine.

Artwork was virtually nonexistent in this system. One exception was a series of ceramic mosaic bas-reliefs erected in some stations. Each featured a simple stone carving linked to the name of the street above or to a nearby landmark. Examples include a bas-relief of Christopher Columbus's flagship, the *Santa Maria*, at the Columbus Circle Station; and of the early American steamboat the *Clermont* at the Fulton Street Station, named for the boat's inventor. At the 116th Street Station, near the Columbia University campus, a carving of the school's official seal decorated the station wall. On the wall of the Astor Place Station was the image of a beaver gnawing on a tree, reminding subway passengers of New Yorker John Jacob Astor's nineteenth-century domination of the fur trade of the early American West.

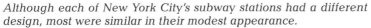

Although each of New York City's subway stations had a different design, most were similar in their modest appearance.

disarray. The sites were often littered with piles of building materials including brick, cast iron pipe, and railroad ties and rails for tracks, as well as various temporary buildings such as tool-sheds, dynamite storage shacks, and shelters for construction bosses and various on-site engineers. Many photographs reveal bombed-out sites with excavated rubble of dirt, stone, and general debris scattered about along with brick foundations, splintered wooden support beams, and the ever-present wheelbarrow crews whose responsibility it was to remove the rubble, guiding their single-wheeled loads up rickety, wooden gangplanks.

On some fortunate streets, normal traffic was never inconvenienced. On certain thoroughfares, such as the busy downtown Park Row, subway laborers built a temporary wooden bridge over the work site, allowing the normal traffic flow of pedestrians, horsecars, and delivery wagons to continue undisturbed.

Makeshift bridges allow subway workers to excavate the 94th Street tunnel without inconveniencing traffic along the busy route.

Subway workers excavate the site of the Union Square tunnel. Most construction sites were littered with wooden support beams, piles of building materials, and temporary sheds and buildings.

NEW CARS FOR THE NEW SUBWAY

While work progressed on the subway line, others were busy designing and building the cars and engines that would travel the newly laid tracks. The first contract for the building of subway cars went to the Wason Manufacturing Company of Springfield, Massachusetts. These cars were made of both wood and steel. For this reason, they were generally referred to as "the Composites." Author Brian Cudahy describes these handsome originals:

> Good looking cars both inside and out, their white ash exteriors were finished in a deep rich wine color. The sides of the cars were slightly tapered, making them narrower at the top than at the bottom. They measured fifty-one feet, two inches in overall length, and just a fraction of an inch over twelve feet high. Each car was equipped with fifty-two seats made of attractive rattan.

Wason delivered two prototypes to the city before a final contract was signed. These cars—named the *August Belmont* and the *John B. McDonald*—were sent to Parsons and his crew

MAYOR McCLELLAN THE MOTORMAN

The October 27, 1904, ceremonies marking the official opening of the New York subway included an event that was not part of the original program. It involved the city's mayor, who, contrary to plan, took the controls of the first official subway train and refused to surrender them until he had played motorman. As it turned out, his unwitting passengers were in for the ride of their lives.

It all started innocently enough. Mayor George B. McClellan was on hand for the dedication ceremonies on that October morning. He and other city officials as well as various subway bigwigs had gathered at city hall for a series of orations and dedications. August Belmont, John McDonald, and others listened attentively as Mayor McClellan delivered a speech in which he declared: "Now I, as Mayor, in the name of the people, declare the subway open." Following that pronouncement, August Belmont stepped forward and handed McClellan a wooden case that contained an ornamental silver subway car controller created by Tiffany and Company. As he handed over the controller, Belmont spoke to the mayor: "I give you this controller, Mr. Mayor, with the request that you put in operation this great road, and start it on its course of success and, I hope, of safety." Before the day was over, Belmont no doubt regretted his words.

Around two o'clock that afternoon, the party of city and subway officials applauded the last of the day's speeches and then walked over to the city hall subway station to take an official ride. At that point the day's true drama began. Mayor McClellan was supposed to operate the inaugural

of engineers early in 1902. They were approved, but saw no regular passenger service. In the summer of 1903, the first production models were delivered, and by fall a total of two hundred cars had been shipped to New York.

To the average New Yorker, these new subway cars were impressive. For one thing, they were four feet longer than the cars used on the elevated rail lines above Manhattan. Other features included hard maple floors and mahogany woodwork. The cars' windows were double-sashed and could be opened at passengers' convenience. Each window unit had its own roll eight-car subway train only for a short distance and then surrender the motorman's control. However, the stubborn mayor had other plans: After attaching the silver controller, he was ready to play motorman. Subway officials soon discovered it was easier to give the control to the mayor than it was to take it away from him. With a jolt, the special eight-car train was off, with the mayor of New York at the helm.

Standing nervously next to Mayor McClellan during his subway joyride were IRT vice president E. M. Bryan and the subway's general manager, Frank M. Hedley. Nervousness turned to alarm as McClellan took their train farther and farther past his handoff point. Indeed, the mayor seemed to be testing just how fast the subway train could go. Historian Clifton Hood describes the scene: "At a point near Spring Street, Hedley tried to coax McClellan into ending his joyride by asking, 'Aren't you tired of it? Don't you want the motorman to take it?' 'No, sir!' McClellan replied. 'I'm running this train!'"

George B. McClellan

McClellan's short career as subway motorman was a bumpy one: At one point in the ride, the mayor accidentally pulled the emergency brake, jerking the train violently to a screeching stop "that sent the silk-hatted, frock-coated dignitaries flying through the air." The mayor, however, merely shrugged off the mishap, increased the speed, and remained at the helm until 103rd Street. A trained motorman then took the controls and finished the trip to 145th Street and back to city hall.

shade. The interior hardware—including the locks, handles, sash fittings, railing brackets, and window guards—was bronze. A row of six electric lights ran the length of each car's ceiling. Twenty additional lights were located above the passenger seats, in two rows of ten. Finally, the cars featured two rows of suspended leather strap loops from one end of the center aisle to the other, for passengers who failed to get a seat to grab while standing.

Unique to the Composites was the positioning of the motorman's station. On these first subway vehicles, the motorman's

Railroad cars carrying Mayor George B. McClellan (right) and other dignitaries return to the City Hall Station after previewing the first completed section of the New York City subway.

station was placed on the car's end platform in a separate compartment with its own door. No longer could talkative passengers distract a busy motorman trying to do his job.

These cars proved both very durable and well suited for use on the New York City subway system. They remained in use on the subway's original lines until 1916, when they were transferred to New York's older elevated lines. Many of them completed nearly a quarter century of service before being retired. In all, twenty-five hundred such cars were used on the subway at various times. They were the only wooden cars ever used on New York's subway.

ALL-STEEL SUBWAY CARS

Despite the success of the Composites, plans were in the works for all-steel cars for the new subway. The Interborough Rapid Transit Company worked on its own all-steel model for more than a year, completing a prototype in December 1903. It was delivered for service in February 1904, less then a year before the subway opened. Work soon commenced on two hundred such cars. These steel models were a step forward in subway car design. Heavier than the largely wooden Composites, the steel cars could withstand a wreck better and were therefore safer.

ELECTRIC POWER FOR THE SUBWAY

By early 1904, the majority of the work on the subway was completed. As early as New Year's Day, a group of New York dignitaries, including Mayor George B. McClellan, rode a hand-powered car over the nearly finished subway. In April, August Belmont and other subway officials rode the line in a series of cars pulled behind a smallish, oil-burning steam engine. It was not until September that electricity was delivered to the system through a gigantic power plant constructed at the corner of 11th Avenue and West 58th Street. Only then was a regular Composite subway train sent down the line, again with Belmont leading a crowd of subway inspectors, reporters, and city officials.

To provide enough electricity to power all the trains of the New York City subway, the IRT built its own electric plant. This power-generating facility stood on the banks of the North River and was, at that time, the largest electric plant in the country. The great engines and electric generators inside the plant were capable of producing approximately 100,000 horsepower when operating at full capacity and under normal running conditions. Coal powered the plant. Four gigantic turbo generators were installed on the ground floor. These four generators fed alternators that directed the current of electricity at a rate of 7,200 alternations per minute.

THE IRT'S ORIGINAL SUBWAY ROUTE

Although New York's first subway was less than twenty miles in length, the choice of those twenty miles was one of its most successful features. Subway planners had either shown great foresight or been extremely lucky in their choice of routes, for the subway served the mass transit needs of New Yorkers not only in 1904 but also for years to come. The original route was not merely a straight line running from one end of Manhattan to the other. It began at the south end of the island beneath city hall. Here the line was a single-track "turnaround loop." Within a mile of city hall, the line mushroomed from one to four tracks near the Brooklyn Bridge Station. From there the subway moved north under streets that, in 1900, included Park Row, Center Street, New Elm Street, Elm Street, Lafayette Place, 4th Avenue, and Park Avenue, where the subway connected—at the corner of Park Avenue and 42nd Street—with the famous Grand Central Station, one of the most important and spacious of the line and an architectural landmark in its own right. There the subway was connected with another rail system above ground. The station—home of the New York Central and Hudson River Railroads—had been built by famed New York railroad man Cornelius Vanderbilt in the 1860s. (It was not the building standing today: Today's Grand Central was finished in 1913, a building now flanked by skyscrapers including the Pan Am Building and the Chrysler Building.)

At the intersection of Park Avenue and 42nd Street, the subway turned ninety degrees to the west, running beneath 42nd all the way to the then newly named Times Square, after the opening of new offices by the *New York Times* daily newspaper. Here the line turned north again, following the course of

Building materials litter the ground during the building of the Brooklyn Bridge Station in 1904. From this station, three lines of track continued on to 145th Street, while a fourth line joined other tracks heading toward Central Park.

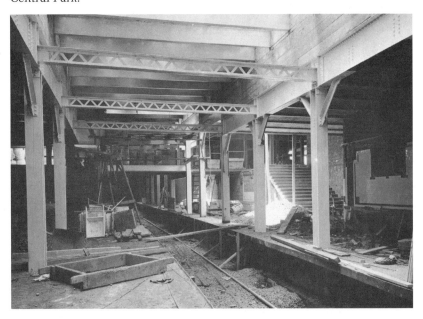

*Carriages and omnibuses congregate near the famous Grand Central Station in this pho-
tograph taken sometime around 1900. The spacious station became one of the most important stops on the new subway route.*

Broadway. The street meanders westward as it travels toward
the northern end of Manhattan, and the subway followed the
same shifting and curving route. Few people in 1904 antici-
pated the importance of the subway station at Times Square;
originally it was only a local stop on the line, with express
trains bypassing it altogether. In time, the Times Square Station would be one of the busiest of the line.

Nearly all of this portion of the line, including the section of
the subway that followed Broadway to 145th Street, was constructed underground. Only a fifteen-block stretch near 125th
Street was built above ground, following a viaduct, to cross a
massive land depression that geologists refer to as Manhattan
Valley. Burrowing under this low point in the landscape would
have required the subway to travel deep underground. To save
time, energy, and money, the IRT decided to build the subway
above ground.

This, then, was the route, from city hall to 145th Street, of
the line that was completed and opened for business after the
official dedication. Later, the tracks were continued north of
145th Street, taking the subway to the very northern end of
Manhattan.

Three of the four lines of track that began at the Brooklyn Bridge Station, at the southern end of Manhattan, continued as far as 145th Street. At 96th Street, the fourth line split off to form a junction. From there, the subway ran east, then cut diagonally northeast through the northern end of Central Park. There the line turned north again, following a route beneath Lenox Avenue and the Harlem River to the borough of the Bronx.

OPENING THE SUBWAY FOR BUSINESS

Though the first New York subway was complete and ready for its first passengers, the public remained skeptical about the safety of underground travel. The IRT held publicity events for several weeks to show the public that their fears were greatly overblown. Historian Stan Fischler describes a portion of the IRT's strategy:

A ticket clerk stands at his post in the South Ferry Station. The IRT adopted the slogan "To Harlem in Fifteen Minutes" in an effort to win public support and build its ridership.

IRT promoters were acutely aware that the public might fear suffocation in the depths of their tunnels. To allay these fears, the subway barons launched a propaganda campaign, distributing timetables which boasted in huge letters: SUBWAY AIR AS PURE AS YOUR OWN HOME. This was followed by more propaganda in the form of an impartial study conducted by Columbia University professor C. F. Chandler, supporting the theory that the air underground was as healthy as surface air.

To drum up public support for the new subway, transit officials had begun using the slogan "To Harlem in Fifteen Minutes," reminding the citizens of New York of at least one of the advantages of subway travel. (By comparison, a trip from Manhattan's southern end north to Harlem on foot would take hours.) That slogan became a reality when a train carrying journalists completed the trip in less than eleven minutes. Rapid transit had indeed come at last to New York City.

Anxious New Yorkers crowd inside a newly completed subway tunnel during the official opening of the system on October 27, 1904.

The IRT designated October 27, 1904, as the opening day for their new subway line, and planned the hoopla accordingly. The appointed day was packed with special events, speeches, and first-time rides on the subway. Hundreds of people gathered at city hall to hear speeches honoring those responsible for the subway's financing and construction. Dignitaries present for the dedication ceremonies included Belmont, Parsons, and McDonald.

That evening the line was officially opened. Tens of thousands of eager New Yorkers crowded into the line's underground stations, creating "indescribable scenes of crowding and confusion, never before paralleled." The New York *Tribune* recorded the event the following morning:

> Men fought, kicked and pummeled one another in their mad desire to reach the subway ticket offices or to ride on the trains. Women were dragged out, either screaming in hysterics or in a swooning condition; gray haired

men pleaded for mercy; boys were knocked down, and only escaped by a miracle being trampled underfoot. The presence of the police alone averted what would undoubtedly have been panic after panic, with whole-sale loss of life.

At some stations along the line, policemen had to be sent in, wielding their nightsticks to help break up the crowds. It is es-timated that nearly 150,000 eager New Yorkers took their first subway ride on the evening of October 27, 1904. Three days after the subway opened, great crowds of New Yorkers, and the curious from outside the city itself, converged on the sub-way for a Sunday afternoon ride. Nearly 1 million people at-tempted to gain access to the underground line that day. Officials of the IRT were relieved to see that, despite a common fear among New Yorkers that the subway contained "foul or poison" air, the new, subterranean, rapid transit system was an immediate hit with street-weary New York passengers.

PRIVATE PARTY, PUBLIC THOUGHTS

On the evening of opening day, a private party was held in a reserved ballroom to pay tribute to August Belmont, the man who had financed the construction of the subway. Silver medals bearing his portrait—as well as those of Mayor McClel-lan and the president of the Board of Rapid Transit Railroad Commissioners—were given to all in attendance. Those pre-sent knew that Belmont had played a significant role in the creation of New York's first subway. Yet even then Belmont un-derstood that the subway just completed was already inade-quate for New York's rapid transit needs.

Perhaps the builder and contractor of the subway, burly Irishman John McDonald, stated best what he, Parsons, and Belmont had accomplished:

Having shoveled and blasted this four-track highway 54 feet wide under the most crowded part of New York, we have demonstrated that the rapid transit problems of the metropolis can be completely solved. It is now sim-ply a question of more tunnels. There is not a street in the city that cannot be tunneled. . . . I think we have made a beginning of an underground city.

To a great extent, McDonald's prediction proved true. Over the decades since the 1904 opening of the New York City subway, hundreds of miles of subway tunnels have been added to the sprawling subterranean system. Through the efforts of financier August Belmont, subway planner and architect William Barclay Parsons, chief contractor of the line John B. McDonald, and thousands of engineers and unnamed and unsung immigrant laborers, New York's first subway had been built and proved to be a greater success than any one of them had imagined.

Underground Partnership: The IRT and BRT Expand the Line

Before the new subway opened in October 1904, some doubted how well New Yorkers would take to this subterranean form of transportation. However, once the system opened for business, the subway was an immediate success from one end of Manhattan to the other. Subway patrons regularly crowded every available train, especially the express lines that bypassed local stations, whizzing passengers across greater distances in less time. New Yorkers were proud of their subway. It ran efficiently and on time. If anything, the biggest criticism was that there were simply not enough trains running to accommodate the thousands of people who wished to use the subway. In a February 1906 article for *Iron Age* magazine, writer S. D. V. Burr noted the success of this new mass transit system:

> The subway was adopted so quickly by the people and has been so successful during the first year of operation that it is quite probable that there will be some competition when bids are asked for extensions to the system. Instead of the city having something to sell that no one will buy, there will be demand for privileges to be granted.

Ridership on the new subway soon surpassed any subway official's expectations. By design, the subway was intended to carry approximately 600,000 passengers daily, but ridership topped that figure by October 1905. The number of people using the subway continued to rise for years to come. As early as 1908, 800,000 passengers rode the subway each day.

The IRT was a gold mine for financier August Belmont. Within months of its October opening, the IRT was running at an 8 percent profit rate. Such profits were dependent, however, on the IRT's status as the only company running a subway and on high public use. A popular phrase of the day stated this reality in six words: "The profits are in the straps," a reference to the hanging handholds provided for standing-room-only passengers.

In the months following the October opening, additional lines were completed and opened for passenger service. The Broadway line, north of 145th Street to 157th, opened on November 5. The Lenox Avenue line and the Broadway and 96th Street to 145th Street line opened on November 20. Six days later, additional mileage from 149th Street and 3rd Avenue following Westchester Avenue and Boston Road in the Bronx to 180th Street was opened. Additional links were opened in 1905 and 1906, including a line from

New York's subway was an immediate success. So many passengers flocked to the trains that the system was expanded to accommodate the increased ridership.

145th Street to the Bronx through tubes built under the Harlem River and the final leg of the Broadway line from 157th Street to Kingsbridge.

GENERAL MANAGER FRANK HEDLEY

Much depended on the trains' running on time and the system's smooth operation; to that end August Belmont had hired Frank Hedley as the general manager. Hedley brought much skill and many sensible ideas to running the IRT lines. To ease the problem of crowded passengers' jostling one another to board subway cars, he ordered subway cars with multiple doors. To cut costs, he ordered train motormen to switch off their motors and coast where possible. Early on, he replaced human fare collectors in the subway stations with turnstiles into which passengers could drop their nickels, thus eliminating petty theft by nickel-nabbing agents.

To help meet demand, Hedley set up his eight-car express trains on tight, regular intervals, with trains timed five minutes

OVERCROWDING AND SEXUAL HARASSMENT ON THE SUBWAY

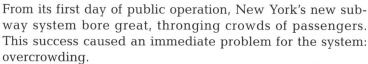

From its first day of public operation, New York's new subway system bore great, thronging crowds of passengers. This success caused an immediate problem for the system: overcrowding.

During peak rush-hour periods when hundreds of thousands of workers crammed their way into the subway on their way to and from work, passengers competed for seats. The early Composite cars featured fifty-two rattan seats arranged along both outer sides of the cars. Despite the illumination of twenty-six electric bulbs, the interiors were dimly lit. Author Clifton Hood presents an unpleasant picture of a typical ride on the New York subway of 1904:

> The cars were very uncomfortable during peak periods when riders competed for seats or hung on to the leather straps, trying to keep their footing on the maple-slatted floors. The straphangers were crammed rudely together with embarrassingly little room to spare, shoulder pressing shoulder, hips jamming buttocks and crotches. The discomfort of the straphangers was aggravated because many passengers refused to move to the center after entering a car; instead they remained near the doors at the ends of the car in order to be the first to exit. This antisocial behavior appears to have been especially common on the expresses. The faster the trains moved, the more quickly New Yorkers wanted to get to their destinations and the more intolerant they became of even the slightest delay. . . . No wonder cynics compared the trains to sardine cans and cattle cars.

While overcrowding in general was a problem, many female patrons of the subway experienced unique discomfort. Often women felt sexually harassed on the underground. One contemporary magazine article charged that women passengers experienced "a crowding which at best is almost intolerable and at its worst is deliberately insulting." The same magazine considered the sexual contact—which was politely referred to as "jostling"—"a violation of the laws of decency."

In response to the problem, the Women's Municipal League suggested in 1909 that the IRT reserve the last car of each subway train for women only. The IRT refused, but another line operator, the Hudson and Manhattan Railroad, agreed. H&M operated a subway between New York City and New Jersey. In April, H&M began reserving a car on each train for women between the hours of 7:30 and 9:00 a.m. and 4:30 and 7:00 p.m. Many women took advantage of this opportunity to ride with other women.

But the practice did not last long. Almost immediately, a fierce debate over whether women should be provided separate transport from men developed, with several women's rights groups lining up in opposition to the H&M plan. By July, the great experiment was over. H&M yielded to the public pressure and once again opened all its subway cars to both men and women. Once again, the women who ventured to ride on New York's subway were forced to fend for themselves.

A sign on the wall of this crowded subway car reads, "This car reserved exclusively for women." During the rush hours, the Hudson and Manhattan Railroad reserved cars for female passengers to keep them from "jostling" with male riders during crowded trips.

Frank Hedley proved to be an able manager of the IRT lines. His innovations helped cut costs and keep the system running smoothly.

apart. Trains were spaced four minutes apart during morning rush periods between 7 and 9:30 A.M. and during the evening rush hour. Local trains (which comprised only five cars) ran on three-minute headways all day, from 5:30 A.M. to midnight. Through the remainder of the night, local trains ran at five- to ten-minute intervals. Despite Hedley's best efforts, however, the subway schedule was not adequate. Clearly, something had to be done to solve the problem.

SUCCESS LEADS TO EXPANSION

Early in 1905, plans were underway for additional lines, including tracks to Brooklyn. Over the next seven years, plans continued for the construction of forty-five miles of subway lines, with a projected cost of nearly $150 million. Most of these new contracts for construction were intended for the IRT.

But, on March 2, 1911, the Brooklyn Rapid Transit Company (BRT) stepped in with a proposal. The BRT hoped to break the

IRT's monopolistic hold over the subway. The BRT proposed a subway line from the southern end of Manhattan Island that included tunneling under Broadway to 42nd Street and up 7th Avenue to 59th Avenue. A second BRT proposal included the construction of a tunnel connecting Brooklyn and Staten Island, making possible a subway line into Richmond County (Staten Island). On March 19, 1913, New York's Public Service Commission issued contracts to both subway companies that would come to be known as the Dual (IRT-BRT) Contracts.

THE ROUTES OF THE DUAL CONTRACTS

The proposed subway lines carried an estimated price tag of $300 million, with the IRT's tab standing at $140 million. The new lines of the Triborough System—which would connect the three boroughs of Manhattan, Bronx, and Brooklyn— added up to 144 miles of single-track construction. Part of the proposed expansion was designed to relieve traffic congestion across the East River between Manhattan Island and Brooklyn by adding routes through Brooklyn's fastest-growing neighborhoods, including Brighton Beach, Astoria, West End, and Sea Beach.

The system envisioned was enormous. The expansion would bring the total number of subway miles to over six hundred. The number of trains in the system would more than double, from 352 to 851. Within seven years of the signing of the Dual Contracts, the IRT and BRT had built enough lines to make the New York City subway system the longest in the world, surpassing London's Underground.

CONSTRUCTION OF THE NEW LINES

By all accounts the original 1904 IRT subway was a grand success, but mistakes had been made during its construction. The planners of the new lines attempted to avoid repeating the IRT's previous errors. For one, construction on the earlier line had involved prolonged dismantling of New York's streets, which disrupted business on those blocks marred by building sites. This time, construction plans called for all cut-and-cover sites to be immediately covered over with a provisional wooden structure, allowing street-level traffic to continue with minimal interruption. This step satisfied merchants and various businesses whose offices lined construction sites.

THE BRT's ROLLING STOCK

While construction progressed on the Dual Contract project, BRT engineers and machinists were busy designing the rolling stock to be used on their new lines. Their plans and designs resulted in the building of a subway car which "proved to be as fine and durable a piece of railway rolling stock as this world has seen," writes railroad historian Brian Cudahy. Cudahy gives a description:

> In August 1913 the BRT sent plans to the PSC for a distinctive new car, strongly influenced by the imaginatively designed Boston Elevated Railway cars on the new Cambridge subway. The main difference from the older IRT model was that instead of having doors in the end vestibules, the new car had three sets of twin doors spaced along the side of the car, dispensing entirely with vestibules. The doors were opened and closed by an electro-pneumatic system operated by a conductor from the center of the car.

Known as the Standard, these new BRT-designed cars had other features which set them apart from the IRT's rolling stock. The Standards measured sixty-seven feet in

In March 1915, the BRT unveiled its new rolling stock. The car was called the Standard, and both its interior and exterior differed slightly from the previous IRT models.

New York Transit Museum Archives, Brooklyn

New York Transit Museum Archives, Brooklyn

The longer, wider design of the Standard model (pictured) made it impossible for the car to travel through the smaller IRT tunnels.

length, compared to the IRT's fifty-one-foot-long cars, and measured over a foot wider. American Car and Foundry received the contract to build hundreds of these cars. When finished, the outer body of the cars was painted a deep brown with a black roof. While the first IRT cars were wood and steel—the Composites from a decade earlier—these new BRT cars were all-steel models. These well-designed vehicles saw decades of service on the BRT and later BMT tracks. Their basic structure changed very little during more than a half century of service. The first Standards were rolled into service on the Dual Contract system in March 1915.

The difference in the sizes of BRT and IRT subway cars was only one of the obvious differences between the two companies' lines. During construction, little was done to encourage uniformity between the two subway systems. The two lines were indeed two lines, with only a small number of stations connecting them. Each company designed the hallways and passages leading to the other company's stations to be as narrow and confusing as possible. In addition, since the BRT's cars were bigger than those of the IRT, they were too large to pass through most IRT tunnels.

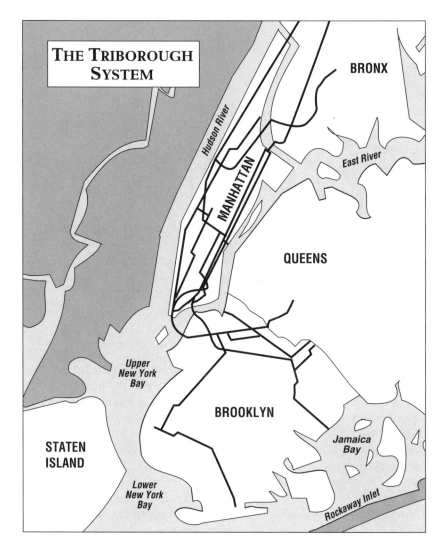

THE TRIBOROUGH SYSTEM

Hudson River

MANHATTAN

BRONX

East River

QUEENS

Upper New York Bay

BROOKLYN

Jamaica Bay

STATEN ISLAND

Lower New York Bay

Rockaway Inlet

The technologies and construction methods used on the new subway lines were not much different from those used in building the 1904 system. Tracks were laid either by the cut-and-cover method, through the carving of new tunnel systems, or as aboveground lines that were built over bridges and viaducts. Tunnel construction was extensive in this phase of New York's subway building. Five new tunnels were built, nearly all featuring twin-tube borings, meaning the tunnels consisted of two separate tubes, one each for trains traveling to and from the three boroughs.

As did the earlier subway, these lines featured construction of four-track tunnels. In most tunnels, the tracks were laid side by side. A unique feature of the Dual Contract phase was the tunnel design for the upper Lexington Avenue line. Here, tracks were laid on two levels, with local tracks running above the express lines. The same two-tiered tunnel system was incorporated in a section of the IRT's line through Brooklyn, with one difference. Local and express tracks going in the same direction were placed on one level, while tracks for both services bearing trains headed in the opposite direction ran on the second level.

TUNNELING UNDER NEW YORK'S RIVERS

Subway construction, always a dangerous business, was most hazardous during construction of tunnels running beneath the rivers—including the Harlem, East, and Hudson—that serve as the natural dividers of New York City's five boroughs. Prior to the Dual Contracts, two underwater tunnels were in use. When the Dual Contract phase was completed, eight new tunnels ran under the Harlem and East Rivers.

Sandhogs—the men who built the tunnels under New York's rivers— labored under hazardous conditions. Here, a group of sandhogs works in one of the tunnels extending under the East River.

The sandhogs—those workers who dug the tunnels beneath the East, Hudson, and Harlem Rivers—toiled under dangerous conditions. They had to walk down dimly lit stairways to a narrow corridor, which was muddy and littered with air and water pipes and other construction equipment. Author Clifton Hood elaborates:

> Far out under the East River they entered at the air lock, an iron chamber that divided the zone of regular atmospheric pressure from that of compressed air. When the air pressure inside the lock equaled the pressure at the end of the tunnel, the men resumed their journey. Beyond the lock, the air was stuffy, moist, and warm. Finally, the workers came to the place where . . . gangs drilled holes for the dynamite, triggered the charges, cleared the mud, sand, and rock that had been dislodged by the blast, and assembled the tunnel's wall.

To make matters worse for sandhogs tunneling under the East River, the riverbed's geology was unstable. For the most

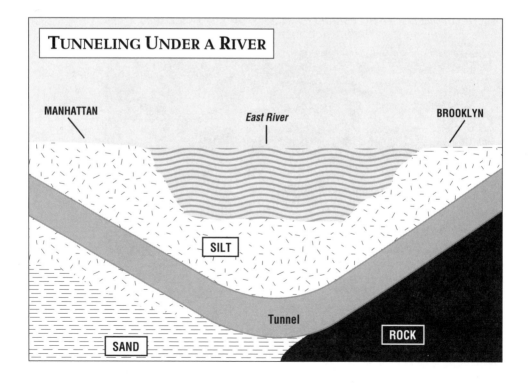

part, the riverbed east of Manhattan was gneiss rock, nearly as hard as granite. However, the gneiss rock was not always solid. At some places, the rock was riddled with cracks and fissures, badly scaled, and laced with gravel, mud, and quicksand deposits. In many instances, sandhogs hammered and blasted through a solid core of gneiss rock only to encounter a weak pocket of unstable rock. Here a sudden break could send river water pouring into the tunnel, trapping and drowning the sandhog miners.

Such an accident occurred in 1906, during work on the Steinway Tunnel, which ran from 42nd Street in Manhattan under the East River to Queens. Nearly three dozen workers were hammering, chiseling, and blasting through a section of gneiss rock when they broke through a massive deposit of soft gravel and sand. The *New York Times* of July 3 reported the accident through the eyes of a surviving sandhog:

> Sand or ground-up stone began pouring in at about 10 [A.M.], and the tunnel lights grew dimmer. Then came a little stream of water, and it kept getting bigger, until finally a big heap of sand and rock came in and we knew that we had hit a shelf of sand. . . . Then came a hissing sound, and we knew that the water was coming at us. One of the men shouted "Danger!"

The workers reacted immediately. At a depth of one hundred feet below the river bottom and over two hundred feet from the tunnel exit, their best strategy was to run to higher ground inside the tunnel. With water pouring in, the sandhogs made their way out of the passageway as the tunnel lights went out, throwing the man-made cavern into pitch blackness. Miraculously, all the workers found their way to safety. Sandhogs and repair crews spent three weeks cleaning up the mess and repairing the damage before tunneling could begin again.

Similar mishaps occurred throughout subway construction, sometimes with disastrous results. In 1905, during construction of an early East River tunnel, a tunnel wall broke, causing the tunnel's airlock to decompress, much the same way a balloon deflates when air is released through the balloon's neck. In his book *Uptown, Downtown*, historian Stan Fischler relates the unlikely survival of one sandhog:

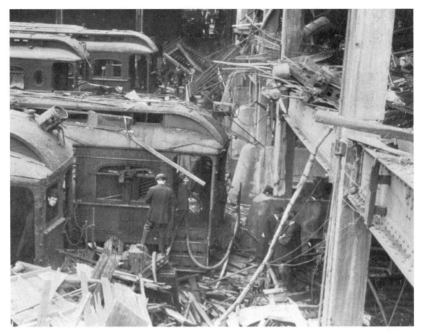

Men rummage through the wreckage of subway cars inside New York's Central Tunnel. Although unusual, accidents and mishaps continued to occur even after the construction was completed.

As the compressed air began escaping a well-disciplined sandhog named Dick Creedon did what he was supposed to do: he snatched one of many available sandbags and rushed to the weak spot, hoping to plug the leak with the sandbag. But Creedon lost his race against time: he was sucked up into the vortex—sandbag still in hand—through thirty feet of river bed and, finally, up through the East River. The sandhog was alive and swimming when a tugboat arrived to haul him to safety. As for the hole in the IRT tunnel, it was plugged after [boats] delivered tons of sand to the leak location and then simply dumped them over the tunnel, where the break soon was repaired.

Such blowouts occurred infrequently. But when they did, lives were often lost and repairs often took weeks. A blowout in the Whitehall Street (Manhattan)–Montague Street (Brooklyn) Tunnel in 1916 killed two men. A third was miraculously spared. The man, Marshall Mabey, was pulled through several feet of thick sand and blasted above the river on a forty-foot geyser of water. Mabey swam to a boat in the river, where he was yanked from the waters of the East River.

Dramatic and deadly mishaps were not limited to the construction phase: Accidents continued even after subway building was completed. Train wrecks, like construction accidents, were not common but could prove equally deadly. The greatest such tragedy to befall the BRT lines occurred on November 1, 1918, when a subway train barreling down a hill at an estimated 60 mph jumped the tracks at the entrance to the Malbone Street Tunnel. Two of the train's passenger-packed cars slammed into the concrete-lined tunnel wall, killing ninety-eight on board.

MAYOR HYLAN'S ANTI-SUBWAY CAMPAIGN

The Malbone Street accident gave New York City mayor John Hylan a rallying point around which to base his campaign to do away with the two privately owned subway companies. Hylan, who had been fired from his subway motorman's job when a supervisor witnessed him taking a curve at a high rate of speed, believed that the city should own and operate the subways. He nursed his grudge by making life difficult for the two subway companies once he became mayor. For example, the mayor blocked construction of a huge equipment repair shop and train storage yard in Coney Island. Hylan also insisted that the subway companies continue the nickel fare for subway passengers even though the cost of construction, equipment, and salaries had made the five-cent fare inadequate. Rising costs and the five-cent fare limit were slowly killing the two subway companies. Despite heavy use of the subway by millions of New Yorkers and others, the lines were, by the post–World War I years, losing money and lots of it.

DEATH OF THE BRT, BIRTH OF THE BMT

In the face of relentless pressure exerted by Mayor Hylan, high inflation, and the reputation-damaging results of the 1918 Malbone Street wreck, the BRT finally broke. By 1923, the BRT was no more. Another company emerged out of the financial wreck of the BRT: the Brooklyn-Manhattan Transit Corporation,

THE BRT's MALBONE STREET WRECK

The Malbone Street wreck was one of the most tragic subway wrecks in the city's history. The accident involved a
BRT train that was being piloted by a substitute motorman.
BRT motormen had gone out on strike effective the morning
of November 1. On the opening day of the strike, BRT train-
master Benjamin M. Brody ordered a young BRT dispatcher
named Edward Luciano to serve the Brighton line, taking a
five-car train to and from Park Row.

It was on the return trip that disaster struck Luciano,
the BRT, and the passengers aboard his train. This particu-
lar route was a difficult one even for experienced motormen. As the train approached the Malbone Street tunnel
from above ground, danger lay ahead. Just twenty feet
from the entrance to the concrete-lined tunnel the tracks
began an S-curve, swerving dramatically to the right, followed by a sharp left turn just fifty feet later. Company reg-
ulations required motormen to reduce the train's speed to a
maximum of 6 mph.

However, twenty-three-year-old Luciano was not pre-
pared for what lay ahead of him on that fateful day. He was
running late, evening was falling, and he was tired. He re-
peatedly took his train to unreasonable speeds, giving his
one thousand passengers frequent tense moments. At several stations before the Malbone Street tunnel, nearly half
of his passengers got off Luciano's train, distrusting the un-
steady hand at the helm.

Unfortunately for Luciano, his remaining passengers,
and the BRT, he chose that section of the route to attempt to
catch up on his schedule. As Luciano began his approach
downhill to Malbone, his train lurched into high speed.
Later, the substitute motorman estimated his approach to
Malbone at 30 mph. Eyewitnesses on board the train
pegged the train's speed at twice that figure.

As it approached the S-curve, the train lurched off the
tracks. Historian Clifton Hood describes what happened next:

> The first car escaped relatively unscathed, but the next
> two cars hit the concrete tunnel so hard that the sound
> of the impact was heard a mile away. . . . The second
> car, number 80, and the third car, number 109, were

both thirty-two-year-old wooden motorless trailers. The roof and the left-hand side of car number 80 was ripped open, and car number 109 was completely destroyed. Passengers were catapulted out of the two cars and onto the roadbed. Because the train kept moving after it left the rails, the wheels of the fourth and fifth cars ran over the riders who had landed on the tracks. Some were decapitated, some had their arms and legs sliced off. Other passengers who had been riding in the second and third cars were hurled against the tunnel wall. Still moving, the train ground them against the concrete in a horrifying "mill of death," leaving a shapeless mass of human flesh, wood splinters, and metal fragments.

When it was all over, nearly one hundred people lay dead along the tracks, inside the tunnel, and in the twisted, shattered debris that had been a BRT train. In addition to the dead, hundreds of passengers were injured. Luciano, on board the train's first car, emerged from the accident with a few scratches.

In the aftermath of the deadly accident, Luciano, five officials of the BRT, and the future of the BRT in general went on trial. Luciano weakly based his defense on his claim that the train's brakes failed. But justice was not served. The company paid over $2 million in damages to survivors and heirs of those who lost their lives in the tragic and unnecessary wreck. However, all five accused BRT officials, plus the negligent motorman Luciano, were acquitted.

But the BRT itself was not so lucky. The accident had been so shocking and so deadly that it remained in the minds of would-be passengers of the line for years to come. To avoid unpleasant reminders, the company saw to the renaming of Malbone Street to Empire Boulevard (the street's name today). Over time the line slowly lost business, having first lost the confidence of its customers. By 1923, the line was failing, and its last days were spent in bankruptcy court. In the end, the final casualty of the great Malbone Street wreck was the Brooklyn Rapid Transit Company.

New York City mayor John Hylan (center) and hundreds of prominent New Yorkers protest proposed subway fare increases. Hylan, an outspoken adversary of the Dual Contracts, opposed raising the nickel fare, even though the two companies were losing money.

popularly known as the BMT. The BMT inherited the BRT's unfinished projects, obtained contracts for new lines, updated its rolling stock, and expanded the turnstile fare collection system.

In the meantime, a new challenge rose which eventually proved too great for the survival of both companies: the creation of a third contender, a city-owned mass transit system called the Independent Subway System.

4

THE IND: NEW YORK'S LAST GREAT LINE

Every year of John Hylan's term as mayor of New York City, he pushed for further subway construction to be funded, owned, and operated by the city. In September 1922, the mayor issued his plan for a new "independent" subway system. In a pamphlet titled *Mayor Hylan's Plan for Real Rapid Transit*, he stated that the subways should be "planned, built, and operated to accommodate the transportation needs of the people." This could only be accomplished, Hylan said,

through a city-run system. Hylan's plan included the construction of 126 miles of new subway lines. Under his plan, the city would also use approximately 100 miles of existing subway lines operated by the other two companies. Hylan's proposed program carried a price tag of $575 million, with a per mile cost of about $5 million.

Hylan's Independent Subway System (IND) proposal was in immediate competition with another subway plan, this one proposed by the New York Transit Commission, a state planning body. The state also wanted control over the subway. The transit commission proposed the building of a 32.5-mile new system at a cost of over $300 million. The

Mayor Hylan crusaded for a city-run subway system during his tenure. In September 1922, Hylan proposed the creation of the Independent Subway System.

two plans had similarities: Both proposed lines along some of the same routes. Both intended to build a line to Washington Heights at the northern end of Manhattan Island. In addition, both proposals called for a crosstown subway line to Brooklyn.

Despite the similarities, on August 3, 1923, the New York State Board of Estimate approved both proposals. The cost for the Washington Heights and crosstown portions of the subway line was pegged at $54 million. While plans, designs, and engineering logistics were being hammered out, the New York State legislature passed a rapid transit act granting, for the first time ever, authority to the city of New York to build and operate new subways at its own discretion through a newly authorized city commission called the Board of Transportation. This body was soon busy with plans to expand the system, with a public announcement of new subway construction plans coming from city government officials by December 1924.

THE IND'S PLANNED ROUTES

The proposed IND lines would extend into all the boroughs of New York with the exception of Staten Island. The line was to be primarily a giant loop of track. The loop's northern end was to run south of Central Park, then turn south to lower Manhattan. From there, the line was to turn to the east toward Brooklyn, tunneling under the East River south of the Brooklyn Bridge. Once in Brooklyn, the line turned north, creating the eastern side of the great loop. The line extended north into Queens to Queens Plaza. Here the subway completed the loop, turning west, recrossing the East River—a tunnel was to pass under Welfare Island in the middle of the river—and returning to its starting place in Manhattan.

Later additions to the Independent Subway System would include two lines on the northern end of Manhattan, one running through Washington Heights and the other under the Harlem River to Bronx Park (the elaborate Concourse line). Other IND lines were built in Brooklyn and Queens, including the Smith Street line through Prospect Park and on to Coney Island, and the Roosevelt Avenue line across eastern Queens to 169th Street. The final line built for the Independent Subway System was a short line branching off the Roosevelt Avenue system to the New York World's Fair of 1939–1940, located in Flushing Meadow Park. The line provided passenger service exclusively to the World's Fair. When the great international fair was over, the line was dismantled.

CONSTRUCTION BEGINS AGAIN

When work on the IND subway lines began in the spring of 1925, the city of New York had already experienced a quarter century of subway construction. Most New Yorkers viewed this latest project as just one in a series of inconveniences but they also eagerly awaited the opening of new subway routes. Subway workers encountered the same maze of underground telephone lines, sewers, water mains, and pneumatic tubes that had slowed earlier projects. In all, they ran into 18 miles of sewers, 26 miles of water and gas lines, and 350 miles of electric lines. While some aspects of construction had not changed since the turn of the century, construction technology in the 1920s was better than the traditional pick-and-shovel method of earlier days. Many of the power shovels used in the construction of the IND were powerful, gasoline-fueled models that replaced the outdated steam-powered shovels. Old-style steam-powered drills were also replaced with more efficient, high-powered models.

Visitors to the New York World's Fair in 1939 wait for gates to open at the subway ramp. When the fair ended in 1940, the temporary subway line to Flushing Meadow Park was dismantled.

THE ZEPHYR, THE GREEN HORNET, AND THE BLUEBIRD

During its earliest years of mass transit service, the BMT built the first sixty-seven-foot-long cars of any subway line in the city. These grand pieces of rolling stock, measuring ten feet wide, soon became the standard size for subway cars in New York, even on IRT lines.

Among the BMT's later designs was the D-type car, introduced in 1927. This subway car was actually three-car units attached to one another by a sharing of one truck (or set of wheels) between two cars. This design allowed subway passengers to walk between the three connected cars without having to pass through a single door.

The next significant BMT-designed cars were introduced in 1934. Designed by two different companies, the first, dubbed the Zephyr, was built by the Budd Company of Philadelphia. This car was made of lightweight stainless steel, making the car suitable for use on both subway and elevated train lines. Inside, the Zephyr boasted "red leather upholstered seats, bull's eye lighting, and a fancy braking system." A primary drawback to the new, experimental design was the lack of automatic couplers between cars. Such cars had to be joined together by hand. Such a restriction was never corrected and the Zephyr, despite its unique qualities, was only used on one BMT line in Brooklyn.

The second design, built by the Pullman-Standard Company and painted two shades of green, was known as the Green Hornet, the name of a popular radio-mystery hero of the 1930s and 1940s. This car was also referred to as the Blimp because its top was rounded. The Green Hornet was similar to the Zephyr in that both trains were built as five cars connected, or articulated, to one another on six trucks. Unlike the stainless steel Zephyr, however, the Green Hornet was constructed of aluminum, another lightweight metal.

Inside, the Green Hornet was a model of modern subway rolling stock. Historian Stan Fischler describes its unique interior features:

> Whenever the Green Hornet–Blimp entered a tunnel, its lights automatically flashed on and, of course, when it climbed out into daylight, the interior lights turned off. Dulcet-toned chimes signaled the closing doors and in-

direct incandescent lighting made reading easier and more pleasant. Even more enjoyable was the Hornet-Blimp's rapid acceleration and braking powers, not to mention its ability to run both in subways and—because of its light weight—on elevated structures.

Just as popular as the Green Hornet design was a train dubbed the Bluebird Special. Its cars were painted blue and accented with white stripes. The Bluebird was a three-car articulated unit. In addition to spring-suspended motors and magnetic track brakes, this subway beauty had interior features that included a state-of-the-art heating system, bull's eye lighting, and mohair seats. The Bluebird saw duty in the final days of the BMT, beginning in March 1939.

Despite the success of these experimental car designs with the subway-riding public, the days of both the Green Hornet and the Bluebird were short-lived. The Bluebird proved costly to maintain, and the Green Hornet, with its aluminum body, became a victim of World War II. A 1942 metal scrap drive tracked down the Green Hornet in a BMT repair shop, waiting for a needed part. The government requisitioned the crippled Hornet, ending its short career as one of the most popular trains of the former BMT.

The Green Hornet was one of the BMT's most popular trains. Its interior boasted modern conveniences, including incandescent lighting and pleasant chimes that signaled the closing of the doors.

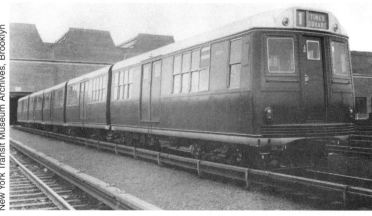

City officials hired thousands of workers to construct new IND tunnels and stations. Here, sandhogs play cards in the tunnels under the East River on November 17, 1931.

Ten thousand men worked on the building of the IND subway and the remaining lines of the IRT and BMT in New York City in the mid-1920s. The majority of sandhogs and street excavators were on IND work sites, which were remarkably accident free. No major cave-ins or massive dynamite explosions marred the IND building project.

Work progressed rapidly. In all, sixteen different construction contracts were under way in 1925 alone. Before the IND was complete, its engineers and sandhogs would clock 7 million ten-hour days.

The scope of the IND project was enormous. In all, 22 million cubic yards of rock and soil were excavated. In his book *Uptown, Downtown*, Stan Fischler estimates that "this material if spread evenly in Central Park would raise its level four feet." He adds that "it would take 198,000 freight cars, comprising a train 1,400 miles long or the distance from New York to New Orleans, to haul this material away."

The new IND included 28 new subway stations, required the pouring of 1 million cubic yards of concrete (representing 6.7 million bags of cement), and used enough steel in the construction of its tunnels to build three Empire State Buildings. The materials used in the building of this massive line came to New York City from all over the United States. Nearly 250 different manufacturing plants, foundries, and mills located in 139 cities representing 13 states provided the steel, cement, wood, and stone for the building of the IND.

As building progressed, city officials grew increasingly grim when they should have been excited. Little progress had been made in uniting the IRT, BMT, and IND into one city-owned subway system. In addition, the five-cent passenger rate had not been increased on any line in the city. According to preconstruction estimates, operating costs of the IND lines would exceed the income generated from the millions of nickels expected to click through the new line's turnstiles. Until the nickel fare was increased, city officials knew that to open the IND for business would mean an immediate cost to the city. Understandably, city officials opened their own subway in the fall of 1932 with rather grim looks on their faces.

OPENING THE IND TO THE PUBLIC

The opening was understated, to say the least; there was little fanfare and no public speeches. John Delaney, chief officer of the Board of Transportation, declared the subway ready for business at midnight on the night of September 10 with the words "Open up" to the guards at the turnstiles of the 42nd Street Station.

Present at the 42nd Street opening was Billy Reilly, a seven-year-old boy born on March 14, 1925, the same day that ground had been broken to mark the beginning of construction on the IND line. Young Billy maneuvered to the head of the waiting throng of would-be subway riders and dropped in the first official five-cent fare. As the Reilly boy slipped through the turnstile, passengers all up and down the new line were paying their nickels as well, bringing the IND into service. Before 1:00 A.M. nearly three thousand eager subway riders had paid their fare and were helping to inaugurate the new twelve-mile-long, city-owned IND line.

In the years that followed, construction continued on the IND lines and additional track was opened to the public every year for the remainder of the decade of the 1930s. The 6th Avenue line, the last major link in the great IND subway chain, was opened on December 15, 1940.

With the end of the 1930s, the greater portion of New York's great subway system was completed. During the first four decades of its existence, various subway designers, planners, and builders had constructed seventy-three miles of subways every ten years. All this had been accomplished through the muscle and enterprise of two private companies, the IRT

A detailed station guide traces the route of the city-owned IND line.

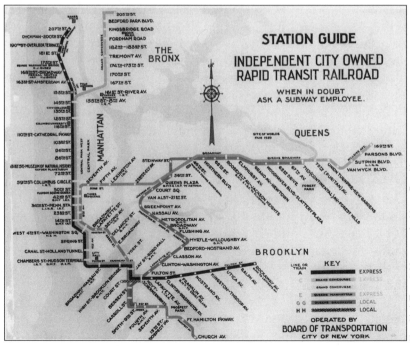

Workmen build a temporary road over the construction site of the 6th Avenue tunnel. This line, the final track built for the IND subway system, was opened to the public on December 15, 1940.

and BMT, joined by the efforts of the latecomer, the IND. Now, all that was left to do was unite those three entities into one.

UNIFICATION OF THE IRT, BMT, AND IND

The year 1940 was significant in New York subway history for another reason. For years, the IRT and BMT had struggled to make a profit, constantly hamstrung by their earlier contracts, which restricted them to a nickel fare for all passengers. In 1932, the year the IND opened for business, the IRT teetered on the brink of bankruptcy. In 1939 and early 1940, respectively, the BMT and the IRT reached fateful decisions. Both companies agreed to sell out to the city-owned IND. In separate agreements, both the BMT and the IRT were scheduled to surrender ownership of their track lines, rolling stock, and equipment in June 1940 to the IND.

The entrance to the BMT's Broadway/Uptown Station. After years of financial difficulties, the BMT surrendered ownership to the city-owned IND in June 1940.

The eras of these two subway pioneers ended within two weeks of each other. The BMT made its last run on May 31. Among the passengers were New York mayor Fiorello H. La-Guardia and his wife, Marie. At 12:01 A.M. on June 1, the BMT became the property of the city of New York. Eleven days later, the last IRT trains ran across the rickety el lines between 2nd and 9th Avenues. By June 12, 1940, New York's subway passengers could no longer ride on lines owned by the IRT. From that date on, they were riding exclusively on trains owned by a newly named system of mass transit: the New York City Transit System. With the establishment of this single operating entity, a grand chapter in the history of New York's subway system was closed.

5

NEW YORKERS AND
THEIR SUBWAY

With the unification of the New York City subway system in 1940, the history of the system took an important turn. Bringing together the separate systems of the IRT, BMT, and IND created an incomprehensibly vast system of tracks. Historian Clifton Hood describes the scope of the newly unified subway system of 1940:

> Unification was a massive enterprise. It constituted the largest railroad merger in U.S. history and the largest financial transaction undertaken by the City of New York. To sign and transfer the checks and legal documents required for the BMT acquisition took an entire morning. . . . The NYCTS was the biggest transit system in the world, a vast network of 760 track miles of subways and els, 435 miles of street railways, and 80 miles of bus lines. It was also the most heavily used system in the world; during its first full year of operation the NYCTS carried a mind-boggling total of 2.3 billion passengers, 1.8 billion of whom were on its subway and elevated lines. . . . On average, every New Yorker took 26.5 trips and spent ten hours riding the system per month. One way or another the transit system touched almost everyone in the city. Without it, New York could not have existed.

With unification, the twenty-six thousand employees of the BMT and IRT joined forces with another nine thousand IND personnel, creating a subway workforce of thirty-five thousand motormen, conductors, token collectors, subway security officers, support people, and subway administrators drawing a total annual payroll of over $60 million. With unification, the New York subway system became wholly owned and operated by the city. In its earliest days, the subway had been constructed and owned by the city, but was leased to private individuals and their support companies, such as August Belmont and the IRT. Leasing provided private operation of the city-owned subway, with the intention that the companies involved would bear the responsibility of maintaining the system, operating its services, turning a profit, and paying the city of New York for the privilege. During the subway's early years, that practice worked fairly well. But as the decades passed, the IRT and BMT found it difficult to operate the system profitably.

For forty years, patrons of the subway paid a mere nickel to use the ever-growing mass transit system. By law, the IRT and BMT had been restricted from raising the subway fare. Yet the value of the nickel declined over time while the costs of operating a large subway system rose. According to some economists, by the 1920s, the nickel that in 1904 provided five cents of income for the IRT system was only worth about half that

Subway conductors and motormen take a break in the crew room. Following unification of the IRT, BMT, and IND lines, the city employed a total of thirty-five thousand subway workers.

New Yorkers pass through turnstiles on their way to the subway. Despite inflation and operation costs, the nickel fare to ride the subway remained in effect for forty years.

amount. Predictably, as profits fell the subway system fell into disrepair. Even by the 1930s, many portions of New York's underground mass transit system were beginning to take on a shabby look. Historian Clifton Hood describes the condition of the subway in the late 1930s, prior to unification:

> The subways were dirty and unattractive. Station benches that had once been painted bright yellow were now worn, chipped, and greasy, while the platforms were often covered with peanut shells, banana skins, candy wrappers, and old newspapers. The trains were old and drab. During the depression, the subways were flooded with homeless people who slept or panhandled there.

Many believed that unification would bring about a new age for the subway system. With the city owning the entire system, profits would rise; ridership would no longer be shared between two private companies and the city of New York. However, this hope remained unrealized.

The Great Depression helped to ruin the IRT and BMT. Between 1928 and 1937, ridership on the IRT dropped by nearly 20 percent and on the BMT by 12 percent, helping to drive the two companies into bankruptcy. By the 1940 unification, the future of New York's subway was in serious doubt.

THE SUBWAY SINCE WORLD WAR II

With the coming of World War II, the downhill slide of New York's subway was halted, at least for a few years. During the war, more Americans had jobs and regular paychecks, giving them money to spend. Gasoline rationing led many New Yorkers to return to the underground by the thousands. (Even by the mid-1940s, two-thirds of New Yorkers still did not own an automobile.) Ridership remained high during the war years. Prior to the war, ridership on the subway had dipped as low as 1.7 billion passengers in 1933. In 1943, 1.9 billion people rode the system, and in 1947 the number rose above the 2 billion mark. Yet, despite the increased ridership, the New York subway system continued to struggle, still hampered by the low fare of a nickel a ride.

With the war's end, the number of passengers on all of America's mass transit systems—including New York's—slowly declined. The primary rival of the city-owned subway, rail, and bus systems was soon the automobile. The figures are stark. In the fifteen-year period following 1945, the number of passengers on New York's subways, buses, and urban rail systems fell from nearly 2.5 billion annually to 1.8 billion. On the city's subways and elevated lines alone—the heart of the city's rapid transit system—ridership dropped from nearly 2 billion to 1.3 billion. This means that by 1960 the number of people using the city's subway system was down by one-third from its 1945 level. Unfortunately for the city of New York, this trend began just a few years after the entire system became its sole responsibility.

In the late 1940s, the financial drain of New York's immense rapid transit system was partially plugged with the end of the nickel fare. Operating costs of the subway shot up during World War II, including a 27 percent increase in subway workers' wages, and the nickel fare was doomed. When, in

Women walk down the stairway to the City Hall Station platform in this December 1945 photograph. Although subway ridership rose during World War II, the system continued to operate under financial hardships.

1947, despite record ridership on the system, the city faced an $18 million operating deficit, it was decided that the longstanding nickel fare had to go. Beginning July 1, 1948, the cost of a ride on New York's subway system doubled from five cents to a dime. Five years later, the fare was raised to fifteen cents. Yet the deficit trend continued. By the early 1950s, government

COUNTING ALL THAT MONEY

For the first forty years of the New York subway's existence, passengers paid a mere nickel to take a ride. In 1948 the rate doubled to a dime. Fifty years have passed since the first subway fare increase. Subway fares have been raised over a dozen times. By 1985, the fare was $.90; five years later it stood at $1.15. In 1995, another fare increase went into effect, raising the cost of a ride on New York's subway to $1.50. As millions of riders pay their daily fares, the New York City Transit Authority faces another problem besides crowded subway cars, system breakdowns, and crime: counting all that money.

Located in Brooklyn, the NYCTA "money room," as it is popularly called, is actually several counting rooms plus a weighing station for coins. Security is tight here, as closed-circuit cameras scan the rooms, helping keep the subway employees who count all that money honest. In fact, cashiers who count subway receipts must wear special brown and khaki uniforms that have no pockets. They may carry no personal belongings with them into the money room.

In his book *Subway Lives*, author Jim Dwyer describes the daily task of counting money collected on the subway:

> The money room of the New York City Transit Authority is the world's busiest private currency-processing enterprise, receiving, counting, double counting, packing, weighing, and shipping upward of 800,000 "pieces" a day. Most of them are singles. On an average day, 46 percent of the work is one dollar bills: 22 percent is twenties; 20 percent is tens; 12 percent is fives.

officials were wringing their hands over annual operating deficits of $20 million, $30 million, even $40 million.

ENTER THE TRANSIT AUTHORITY

In 1953, along with the fare hike to fifteen cents, the city partially separated itself from the running of the subway by creating the New York City Transit Authority (NYCTA), a public corporation with government connections that could administer its own budget separate from the city government's, thus mak-

Other banking operations count greater amounts—including fares from both buses and subways, the TA handles only $5 million a day, while Citibank, Chase Manhattan, Wells Fargo, and Brinks move between $12 million and $20 million. But they deal in big bills. The subway token booths don't accept anything higher than a $20 note, and their customers rarely have anything larger anyway.

In addition to the paper money, TA cashiers must count millions of dollars in coins weekly. Most of this work is done by Brandt machines, which can sort five thousand coins a minute. However, the process is more time-consuming than it appears: Before coins are thrown into the machines for counting, cashiers must hand sift out foreign coins and slugs, worthless metal imitations that pass for coins when fed into a subway token turnstile.

Many different token designs have been used since the subway first opened in 1904. The coins shown below were used between 1953 and 1995.

ing the government's responsibility to the rapid transit system less direct. The NYCTA technically leased the system from the city of New York and ran the system through a five-member board of directors, four of whom were appointed by the mayor of New York City and the state governor. Such a move also allowed the city to put some distance between itself and a rising chorus of public complaints about the subway's cleanliness, efficiency, and safety. But the move to Transit Authority control of the subway did not solve the system's problems.

New York's subway system has experienced an overall deterioration since the 1950s. Today, subway cars are plagued by graffiti and crime.

Beginning in the 1950s, the New York City subway system has undergone a forty-year decline financially, operationally, and in number of passengers. The NYCTA has never managed to remedy the system's failures. Despite many fare increases, the New York subway remains a financial disaster. Clifton Hood sums up this continuing decline in the final chapter of *722 Miles:*

> The creation of the NYCTA set the stage for the subways' deterioration in the 1970s and afterward. Ridership continued to drop as more New Yorkers took to the highways, and the fare had to be raised ten times between 1953 and 1990. Nine of every ten subway trains had run on schedule during the 1930s and 1940s, but by 1983 on-time performance fell to 70 percent. The average distance a subway car traveled between breakdowns dropped from 34,294 miles in 1964 to 9,000 miles in 1984. Rising crime and graffiti made the system a national symbol of urban violence and disorder. . . . By any measure the subways had hit bottom.

AN UNCERTAIN FUTURE

What will be the future of the New York City subway system in the next century? Many of the problems that have historically plagued the vast underground system remain unsolved today. In the 1980s the NYCTA began a campaign to rebuild the system. Subway cars were either overhauled or rebuilt and subway stations were renovated and cleaned up. Construction crews were sent throughout the system, rebuilding hundreds of miles of track. But many problems continued to present themselves, especially the problem of financing the huge cavernous system of trains and track. The future remains bleak for a rapid transit system on which, ironically, New Yorkers still depend for their urban mobility. This mobility, unheard-of in the New York City of the late nineteenth century, is something New Yorkers have come to rely on in their modern, urban world. Perhaps that very dependence on a century-old system of rapid transit will guarantee the future of that system into the twenty-first century and beyond.

FOR FURTHER READING

Joan Hewett, *Tunnels, Tracks, and Trains: Building a Subway*. New York: Lodestar/Dutton, 1995.

Felice Holman, *Slake's Limbo*. New York: Scribners, 1974.

Tamra Hovey, *Paris Underground*. New York: Orchard Books, 1991.

O. S. Nock, *Underground Railways of the World*. London: Adam and Charles Black, 1973.

L. H. Whittemore, *The Man Who Ran the Subways: The Story of Mike Quill*. New York: Holt, Rinehart & Winston, 1968.

Roger Yepsen, *City Trains: Moving Through America's Cities by Rail*. New York: Macmillan, 1993.

WORKS CONSULTED

Benson Bobrick, *Labyrinths of Iron: A History of the World's Subways*. New York: Newsweek Books, 1981.

Brian Cudahy, *Under the Sidewalks of New York: The Story of the Greatest Subway System in the World*. Brattleboro, VT: Stephen Greene Press, 1979.

Jim Dwyer, *Subway Lives: 24 Hours in the Life of the New York City Subway*. New York: Crown, 1991.

Stan Fischler, *Uptown, Downtown: A Trip Through Time on New York's Subways*. New York: Hawthorn Books, 1976.

Clifton Hood, *722 Miles: The Building of the Subways and How They Transformed New York*. New York: Simon & Schuster, 1993.

Interborough Rapid Transit, *The New York Subway: Its Construction and Equipment*. New York: Fordham University Press, 1991. (Facsimile of a 1904 edition published by the IRT.)

Frederick A. Kramer, *Building the Independent Subway*. New York: Quadrant Press, 1990.

Fred Lavis, *Building the New Rapid Transit System of New York City*. New York: Hill Publishing Company, 1915. (Reprinted from *Engineering News*.)

Rene Poirier, *Engineering Wonders of the World: The Stories Behind the Greatest Engineering Feats in History*. New York: Random House, 1957.

James Blaine Walker, *Fifty Years of Rapid Transit, 1864 to 1917*. New York: Law Printing Company, 1918.

INDEX

American Car and Foundry, 57

Beach, Alfred Ely, 20–21
Beach Transit bill, 21
Belmont, August, 24, 33, 43, 49, 51
Bluebird car, 70, 71
Board of Rapid Transit Railroad Commissioners (RTC)
formation of, 23
Bobrick, Benson, 33
Brooklyn Bridge, 18
Brooklyn-Manhattan Transit Corporation (BMT), 63, 66
last run of, 76
Brooklyn Rapid Transit Company (BRT), 54
demise of, 63
dual contract with IRT, 55
Bryan, E. M., 41
Burr, S. D. V., 50

City Hall Station, 36–37
Composites, 39, 41, 42, 43, 52
Creedon, Dick, 62
Croton Dam project, 23
Cudahy, Brian, 10
on BRT Standard cars, 56
cut-and-cover method, 28–29, 30, 31, 32

Daley, Robert, 14
Dual Contracts, 55
Dwyer, Jim, 82

elevated rail (the el), 16–18, 31

failed as answer to mass transit, 18–19
Epps, Moses, 33, 34, 35

Fenton, Ruben E., 16
Fischler, Stan, 28, 46, 61
on the Green Hornet cars, 70–71

Grand Central Station, 44
Great Depression, 80
Green Hornet car, 70, 71

Hecla Iron Works, 29
Hedley, Frank M., 41, 51
Heins and LaFarge, 37
Harvey, Charles T., 16
Hewitt, Abram S., 19, 22
"Hewitt formula," 19
Hoffman, John T., 21
Hood, Clifton, 11
on condition of subways before unification, 79
on decline of subway system, 84
on Malbone Street wreck, 64–65
on Mayor McClellan's joyride, 41
on overcrowding of subway cars, 52
on subway's initial route, 27–28
on tunneling under rivers, 60
on unification of subway system, 77
on William Barclay Parsons, 26

Hudson and Madison
    Railroad, 53
Hylan, John, 67
    antisubway campaign of, 63

Independent Subway System
    (IND), 66, 67
    construction of, 67
    new stations of, 73
    opening day of, 73–74
    planned routes of, 68
Interborough Rapid Transit
    Company (IRT)
    all-steel cars of, 42–43
    dual contract with BRT, 55
    formation of, 26
    last run of, 76
    opening day of, 40–41,
        47–48
    original route of, 43–46
Iron Age magazine, 50

kiosks, 28, 29

LaGuardia, Fiorello H., 76

Mabey, Marshall, 62
Malbone Street wreck, 63,
    64–65
Manhattan Valley, 45
Mayor Hylan's Plan for Real
    Rapid Transit, 67
McClellan, George B.
    joyride of, 40–41
McDonald, John B., 23, 24,
    26, 48, 49
Metropolitan Railway
    Company, 15
multiple-unit control, 27
Municipal Explosives Com-
    mission, 35

New York City
    boroughs of, 10
    population of
        at end of nineteenth cen-
            tury, 12
        growth, 1840–1860, 14
        prominence of subways in
            life of, 11–12
New York City Transit
    Authority
    creation of, 82–83
New York City Transit
    System, 76
New York Elevated Railway,
    18
New York Transit Commis-
    sion, 67
New York World's Fair of
    1939–1940, 68

Panic of 1893, 23
Parsons, William Barclay, 23,
    26, 27, 28, 49

Rapid Transit Act of 1891, 22
Rapid Transit Subway
    Construction Company
    formation of, 26
Reilly, Billy, 73–74
Robinson, A. P., 15
Roots Patent Force Blast
    Blower, 21
RTC. See Board of Rapid
    Transit Railroad Commis-
    sioners

sandhogs, 59, 60
722 Miles: The Building of the
    Subways and How They
    Transformed New York
    (Hood), 11

Shaler, Ira A., 35
Sprague, Frank, 26, 27
Standard cars, 56–57
    first service of, 57
Steinway Tunnel accident, 61
subway
    cars, designs of, 39
        on BMT lines, 70
    elevated tracks on, 31
    fare increases, 78–79, 80–82
    original routes of
        IRT, 27, 43–46
    overcrowding and sexual
        harassment on, 52–53
    power source for, 26, 43
    prominence in life of New
        York City, 11–12
    public concerns on safety
        of, 46
    ridership on, 13, 50
        during/after World War II,
        80
    stations, design of, 36–37
    uncertain future of, 85
    unification of lines, 75–76
    uniformity between lines, 57
    workforce of, 77–78
Subway Lives (Dwyer), 82

Tammany Hall, 23, 24
Tiger (ship), 33
Times Square, 44, 45
Triborough System, 55, 58
tunnels
    construction of, 28

accidents during, 33–35,
    61–63
barriers to, 32–33, 69
cut-and-cover method,
    28–29, 30, 31, 32
Dual Contract lines,
    58–59
interference with street
    business by, 35, 38
IRT, changes in technolo-
    gy affecting, 69
relics found during, 33
under rivers, 59–63
design of, 30
lighting of, 31
Tweed, William Marcy
    "Boss," 16, 20

Under the Sidewalks of New
    York (Cudahy), 10
Uptown, Downtown (Fischler),
    61, 73

Vanderbilt, Cornelius, 44
Van Wyck, Robert A., 25

Wason Manufacturing
    Company, 39
Whitehall St.–Montague St.
    Tunnel accident, 62
Willson, Hugh B., 14–15, 16
Women's Municipal League,
    53

Zephyr car, 70

PICTURE CREDITS

Cover photos, clockwise from left: Archive Photos, Archive Photos, Corbis-Bettmann

Alexander Alland Sr./Corbis-Bettmann, 45

Archive Photos, 16, 18, 22 (bottom), 47, 51, 62, 76, 84 (both)

Archive Photos/Blank Archives, 83

Corbis-Bettmann, 17, 19, 34, 38, 75

Culver Pictures, Inc., 15, 22 (top), 24, 25, 31, 35, 42, 53, 78, 79

Library of Congress, 8, 9, 11, 28, 36, 37, 39, 41, 44

New York Transit Museum Archives, Brooklyn, 23, 46, 56, 57, 71, 74

UPI/Corbis-Bettmann, 12, 27, 54, 59, 66, 67, 69, 72, 81

ABOUT THE AUTHOR

Tim McNeese received a bachelor's degree from Harding University in Searcy, Arkansas, and a master's degree in history from Southwest Missouri State University. He taught secondary-level history, English, and journalism for sixteen years, and is currently associate professor of history at York College.

He has written twenty books for young readers, including two eight-part series, *Americans on the Move* and *American Timeline*, and four books for the *Building History* series. He coedited the college texts *History in the Making: Sources and Essays of America's Past*, Volumes I and II.

Tim and his wife, Bev, live in York, Nebraska, with their daughter, Summer, and their son, Noah, who attends York College. They share their home with two Siamese cats and a cocker spaniel named Franklin. Tim enjoys woodworking, traveling, reading, and writing.